Socio-Economic Constitutional Rights in Democratisation Processes

Lex et Res Publica

Polish Legal and Political Studies

Edited by Anna Jaroń

Volume 1

PETER LANG

Frankfurt am Main · Berlin · Bern · Bruxelles · New York · Oxford · Warszawa · Wien

Anna Jaroń

Socio-Economic Constitutional Rights in Democratisation Processes

An Account of the Constitutional Dialogue Theory

PETER LANG
Internationaler Verlag der Wissenschaften

Bibliographic Information published by the Deutsche Nationalbibliothek
The Deutsche Nationalbibliothek lists this publication in the Deutsche Nationalbibliografie; detailed bibliographic data is available in the internet at http://dnb.d-nb.de.

Cover Design:
© Olaf Gloeckler, Atelier Platen, Friedberg

This book has been published with a financial subsidy from the European University Institute.

This publication is based on an EUI Ph.D. thesis.

ISSN 2191-3250
ISBN 978-3-631-61901-8

www.peterlang.de

Acknowledgments

Usually, the first and last pages of the book are the most widely read of the entire publication. They are also the most enhanced parts of the work, which reflect its core content. While it may be true to some extent, here is the place where I may take a step back and look at the distance on the theories and arguments I articulated in throughout the pages of this book. Hereby, I want to recognise the foundations that lie at the bottom of this work, without which writing of it would have been impossible.

This book is a result of the research I have conducted at the Department of Law of the European University Institute in Florence. In this place, I want to thank my supervisor professor Wojciech Sadurski for his continuous support during the PhD program at the EUI. He taught me how to ask questions and formulate thoughts. His support to my interdisciplinary approach to the research encouraged my working spirits. I am deeply thankful for the attention I have received from you Professor.

I also want to express my gratitude to constitutional justices I had a pleasure to meet and interview for the purposes of my thesis – prof. Ewa Łętowska, prof. Marek Safjan, prof. Mirosław Wyrzykowski, prof. Jerzy Ciemniewski from the Polish Constitutional Court, and prof. Vojtech Cepl from the Czech Constitutional Court. My thanks go also to Ján Štiavnický, Erika Kurakova and Miloslav Babjak court advisers of the Slovak Constitutional Court, who have been my guides on Slovak constitutional jurisprudence and practice. I also want to thank Ivo Pospíšil, legal assistnat of the Constitutional Court of the Czech Republic; Tomáš Langášek, Secretary General of the Constitutional Court of the Czech Republic; Štěpán Pecháček, Head of General Analyses Division of the Parliamentary Institute in the Czech Republic; prof. Zdeněk Kühn and especially dr Jan Kudrna from Charles University Law School for fruitful and extensive discussions on Czech constitutional system; Michal Bobek my EUI colleague who have introduced me to the Czech constitutional scholarship.

In the writing of my PhD thesis I had a valuable support of my family. In particular, I want to sincerely thank my parents Magda and Andrzej, to whom this book is dedicated. Thank you for supporting my life choices and encouraging me to realise my dreams. I also want to express my heart-felt gratitude to my husband Przemek. Your care and patience helped me to stay focused. Thank you.

Warsaw, September 2011.

To My Parents

Abstract

This book is primarily concerned with examining changes in the conceptual understandings of socio-economic rights in the constitutions of countries that have undergone processes of democratisation. In particular, it focuses on the processes of constitution-building, but most importantly on questions such as justiciability of social and economic constitutional rights and their materialisation in the effective socio-economic policies of democratic states.

Through the examination of theories of constitutional interpretation of these rights in Poland, the Czech Republic and Slovakia, this book explores further the argument for a constitutional intra-institutional dialogue. In this sense, the interpretation of socio-economic constitutional rights is not simply taken from the constitution and made into legislation. Instead, the interpretation is to be seen as a dynamic process between state institutions. It is claimed that only within this process can the constitutionalisation of socio-economic rights take place. In other words the parameters are being set for the ultimate aim of the constitutional formulation of these rights, which is to ascribe them with the attributes of legal rights.

The aim of this book is to discuss the foundations of the continuous process of the realisation and enforcement of socio-economic rights with respect to the cross-penetration of constitutions and ordinary legislations, judicial and non-judicial mechanisms, constitutional judiciary, other constitutional organs, and governmental and administrative institutions, all of which shape the general performance of the countries in the creation and exercise of social and economic policies. Consequently, the claim of the Constitutional Courts' activism in socio-economic adjudication is juxtaposed within the broader concept of constitutional dialogue theory.

Table of Contents

Introduction

Constitutionalisation of socio-economic rights is perhaps one of the most debatable issues within modern constitutional scholarship. The discussions on justiciability and the enforcement of socio-economic constitutional rights are present not only at national levels but also on the international scene with respect to international and regional treaties (International Covenant on Economic, Social and Cultural Rights, European Charter of Social Rights), and most recently at the European Union level (Charter of Fundamental Rights). Essentially, opinions vary as to whether social rights should be attributed with the more concrete nature of individual (subjective) rights, or left as prerogative of each state to shape its social policies.

Yet, the revived interest in socio-economic rights did not go beyond the well known arguments for and against their constitutional justiciability. Commonly, the juxtaposition of *socio-economic rights* with *civil and political rights* has been repeatedly underlined. In this light, socio-economic rights are called "second generation rights" and are presented as weak rights whose materialisation undermines other constitutional rights. According to constitutional doctrine the difference between social and political rights lies in their substance, but also in the fact that *civil and political rights* were recognised before *social and economic rights* were given constitutional grounds. Prior recognition assumes precedence and indicates that the initial rights are more legitimate. The different nature of both categories of rights is also affirmed. This controversy in turn is reflected in the legal argument concerning the opposition of different legal techniques, being on the one hand of protection (civil and political), and on the other of non-interference (social and economic) with concrete rights.

The recent scholarship challenges the above mentioned controversies, and so does this book. The novel perspective that is proposed here draws from constitutional debates during the period of transition to democracy in the early 1990s in Central Eastern Europe. There are several reasons to believe this approach will bring new arguments to the "old" debate. Firstly, the discussions over making socio-economic rights constitutional within the context of transition to democracy highlights the idea of regime change. The transition from communism to democracy confronted the well-established dichotomy between *civil and political* and *social and economic rights* by justifying the grounds for retaining socio-economic rights within the constitutional texts of the new-born democracies. The transition to democracy entailed specific legal undertakings aimed at establishing stable democratic institutions and rules that would determine how the state would function. The aspect of institution-building and the institutional design provides a challenging account of the role of socio-economic constitutional rights. Namely, it is assumed that these rights are more than moral obligations of the state to provide a dignified life for its citizens. It is not simply that they create expectations of citizens upon their state, but also that they create a space for intra-institutional dialogue. By virtue of their complex nature these rights can be considered as a test for democracy. Secondly, the transitional constitutional debates emphasised an important aspect of modern constitutions common to the European Community spirit. Modern democratic constitutions are thought not only to contain a set of regulations that define basic separation of powers and determine the institutional design of the state. Instead, constitutions reflect the idea of a particular society, its organisation and its aspirations. This in turn reflects the modality of the formulation of rights within a given constitutional act and thus indirectly, their materialisation methods. The presentation of the nature of constitutional socio-economic rights in the context of the democratisation and constitutionalisation processes in Central Eastern Europe has yet another important dimension. It provides a foundation for analysis into the evolution of the conceptions of socio-economic constitutional rights. The change in understanding of socio-economic rights mirrors the substantive constitutional reform that brought in the implementation of democratic standards, such as the principle of the rule of law, democratic methods of governance, citizens' participation in political life and the development of transparent legislation. Also, constitutional principles provide a basis for future constitutional adjudication in socio-economic matters. Finally, the European experience confirms that the generational dichotomy between rights was inherently linked to the idea of partition between Western and Eastern European countries- the residues of the post-World-War II division. The recent constitutionalisation of socio-economic rights at the EU level therefore removes the old divisions.

Through the examination of theories of constitutional interpretation in the three selected Central Eastern European countries, this book explores the argument for a constitutional intra-institutional dialogue. In this sense, the interpretation of socio-economic constitutional rights is not simply read off from the constitution but instead, it is viewed as a dynamic exchange of constitutional interpretation between state actors: the executive, the legislator and the constitutional judiciary. The claim that once constitutionalised socio-economic rights become a test for democracy is verified in the light of the conceptual change of the meaning of socio-economic rights. This leads to a discussion of the nature of socio-economic constitutional rights, largely concentrated on their material substance. By placing emphasis on procedural aspects, the foundations for a discussion on realisation and enforcement of socio-economic rights are set. These are based on intra-institutional interactions, which serve materialisation of constitutional socio-economic rights. The cross-penetration of constitutions and ordinary legislations, judicial and non-judicial mechanisms, constitutional judiciary, other constitutional organs, and governmental and administrative institutions, shape the general performance of the countries in the creation and exercise of social and economic policies. Again, socio-economic rights are shown here not as a product of constitutional text. Nor are they given the meaning through interpretation of constitutional courts. Instead, a wider picture of creation of the substantive meaning of constitutional socio-economic rights is drawn. In this picture the plurality of state organs are the interpretors of a particular right. In fact, it is not the sole constitutional interpretation given by constitutional court, but it is also a materialisation of a right that defines it. Consequently, the claim of constitutional courts' activism is confronted with a broader concept of the constitutional dialogue theory.

The choice of representative constitutions of democratised countries was not easy. Almost every country in the region shows its specificities and deserves a separate study. Ultimately, this study concentrates on three Central Eastern European (CEE) countries: the Republic of Poland, the Czech Republic and the Slovak Republic (with reference to the Czechoslovak Republic before the split of 1993). So far, the studies of constitutionalisation and democratisation in CEE encompass the so called Visegrad Four group (Poland, the Czech Republic, Slovakia, and Hungary). The selection of the three countries from the bigger group of the CEE countries is however, important for several reasons. Firstly, such an attempt leads to a more focused research on constitutional socio-economic rights and their subsequent materialisation in the ordinary legislation on public social and economic policy programmes. Secondly, it provides a new perspective for region-oriented study, by leaving aside wide spread classifications and distinctions. Moreover, the common categorisation of the CEE counties as belonging to the same "family" and thus clustered as similar in terms of their constitutional heritage is contested. Indeed, these countries display many similarities in their constitutional, legal, political, social and economic history: they were under the influence of the Soviet regime; accepted the communist political system; introduced Marxist class division and centralised the economy. Although the 1990s brought democratic changes in the three countries at around the same time, the systemic differences in constitutional transformations exerted substantive differences between the countries in the study.[1] The same applies to the constitutional

1 An exemplar is Jiří Přibáň's discussion on application (in Poland) and a resistance to do so (in Czechoslovakia) of the retroactive legislation resulting from the type of transition. Přibáň points out that the reluctance to apply the retroactive legislation was generally higher in 'transitional countries' (ex. Poland) than in 'revolutionary countries' (ex. Czechoslovakia). See:

courts: the way they operate, the interpretative techniques and tools are not identical and therefore the patterns of constitutional adjudication in socio-economic matters vary. Again, although the three countries underwent transition to democracy, their paths were hardly identical. Whereas in Poland constitutional talks lasted several years, the current constitution of the Czech Republic was written almost over-night, while the Slovak constitution was accepted as a result of the Czecho-Slovak Republic split. Attitudes towards heritage within the former regimes also differed. Moreover, the Polish Constitutional Tribunal operated under the constitutional *provisorium*, while the Czech and Slovak Constitutional Courts could directly refer to new, democratic regulations.

This book is divided into three major parts. Part one (Chapter 1 and 2) introduces the concepts of socio-economic rights and offers a separate account of constitutional socio-economic rights. By distinguishing between the two it provides for a detailed analysis of the nature of these rights and gives full explanation of the features they gain once constitutionalised.

Chapter 1 discusses the nature of socio-economic rights. The complex nature of constitutional social and economic rights opens a debate on legal, political, economic and moral justifications for constitutional justiciability of these rights, where several important issues are raised. These are: the relationship between social and economic rights and civil and political rights, the politisation of the judiciary and judicialisation of politics, negative versus positive obligations of the state and its institutions, the extent of welfare policies and state benefits, the resource capacity of the state, a moral claim to demand the right to live in dignity, and many others. However interesting these debates are, they are simply touched upon, as it is beyond the scope and extent of this book to undertake a detailed discussion on each and every issue. Chapter 2 follows with the study of the general nature of socio-economic rights, though in this instance the constitutional socio-economic rights are considered. The central issue of the nature of socio-economic constitutional rights is highlighted most clearly in the distinction between direct enforceability of the constitution versus enforceability dependent upon the legislative discretion. The question of enforceability, therefore, concerns the normative level at which social and economic rights are divided into those constitutionally enforceable and non-enforceable. Such consideration does not have any direct transposition to the question of socio-economic rights' hierarchy or importance. Constitutional enforceability is a way by which certain

---

Jiří Přibáň, Pauline Isobel Roberts, James Young, *Systems of justice in transition: Central European experiences since 1989*, Aldershot, Burlington Vt, Ashgate 2003, p.37 and further.

rights are strengthened and some are assigned to the highest judicial considerations having a bearing on a state's policies through the constitutional review.

Part two (Chapter 3, 4 and 5) of this book presents constitutional debates in the three countries under study and analyses selected case law. Chapter 3 is devoted to the presentation of similarities and differences in constitutional debates in Poland, the Czech Republic and Slovakia. The constitution-making processes are analysed with particular attention to the debates on constitutionalisation on socio-economic rights. Next, in Chapter 4 the issue of change in the meaning of socio-economic rights is analysed. The modality of the constitutional formulation of socio-economic rights is the point at which an in-depth study of the substantial change which socio-economic constitutional rights underwent in the constitutional reforms of the 1990s is embarked upon. Chapter 5 constitutes the fundamental core for the empirical study. It discusses constitutional case law on three selected constitutional socio-economic rights: the right to health care, the right to social security and the right to education. The rationale for such selection was based on the most representative socio-economic cases from the *constitutional acquis* of the three countries under study. Firstly, the right to health was chosen as a right that contains two components: the individual right and the social right (further discussed in sub-chapters 5.1.1 and 5.1.2). Then, the right to social security reflects the ways constitutional courts had to deal with issues stemming from benefits previously allocated through addressing the principle of acquired rights, especially within the context of the altered economic circumstances. Finally, the right to education was selected as an example of a right which has the most distinct cross-sectoral character, i.e. not only it influences a number of spheres of human life, but it is also dependant on the performances of rights protection from other "sectors". The selection of cases of different periods has also allowed to show specific approaches and the use of adjudication techniques by the three courts. The legal state of affair covers the period from the early days of the functioning of the three constitutional courts up until December 2009.

Part three which comprises of Chapter 6 offers an account of deliberations on whether the undertakings directed to the protection and promotion of socio-economic rights provide for exclusiveness or inclusiveness of different state organs. At this point the theory of the constitutional dialogue is referred to. It is claimed that the dialogue rhetoric better suits the actual mode of constitutional socio-economic rights' interpretation. It emphasises the most important task common to all constitutional actors- the materialisation of constitutional socio-economic provisions. Generally, it is argued that the evolution of socio-economic rights' understanding is dependant upon the continuous process of realisation and enforcement of social and economic rights, which is based on a cross-penetration of constitutions on one hand, and on the other of the legislator's actions, judicial and non-judicial mechanisms of rights' promotion and enforcement, governmental and non-governmental actors' activities. It is further assumed that the processes of democratisation together with the consolidation of democracy reveal changing methods and mechanisms of constitutional social-economic rights' concretisation. In fact, these processes illustrate the way in which the meaning of rights changes.

It is expected that despite the differences in formulation of socio-economic rights in the three constitutions, there is little difference in substantive interpretation of socio-economic rights. What is different, however, ought to be the theoretical background the courts use and the strength of the "institutional entourage" that influences the end result of Courts' decisions. It is indeed the "institutional entourage" in which constitutional courts adjudicate, and the analysis of institutional dynamics which lets the courts establish their position among other constitutional bodies, that consequently leads these courts to achieve institutional prerogative to decide in socio-economic matters. Paradoxically, constitutional courts alone are too powerful to exercise their proper power of constitutional review. Yet, not only the institutional checks and balance principle or procedural limits to exercise constitutional courts' functions curtail the courts in a possible arbitrary use of their powers. It is claimed that the constitutional dialogue between the court and the legislator is necessary to overcome this problem.

As a final remark it should be mentioned that the constitutional dialogue is defined in broad terms; meaning that the constitutional courts are assisted by other constitutional institutions who participate in the channelling of the information between the two crucial actors- constitutional courts and the legislator- in order to render the court's decisions as achievable . Considered in this way, constitutional review, or constitutional politics as it is sometimes called, should be seen as a careful deliberation of political interests on one hand, and constitutional premises on the other. The materialisation of justiciable social and economic constitutional rights is not only limited to their formulation in the constitution, but also to the institutional and procedural design of the constitutional review.

PART I

THE NATURE OF CONSTITUTIONAL SOCIAL AND ECONOMIC RIGHTS

Chapter 1
Characteristics of Socio-Economic Rights

1.1 Approaching Socio-Economic Rights

The recognition of social and economic rights understood as an injunction to take care of those in need and those who cannot look after themselves, originates from the major religious traditions. Other sources draw from philosophical and political theories, political programmes developed mainly in the period of the 19th century industrialisation processes, and constitutional precedents, such as the Mexican Constitution of 1917, the following Soviet Constitutions in the Soviet Union and its satellite countries, and also the 1919 Constitution of the Weimar Republic (which introduced the *Wohlfahrtsstaat* concept).[2] When discussing the nature of social and economic rights, the focus on explanation of their content tends to be on provisions provided for in the international human rights treaties, starting with the Universal Declaration of Human Rights (UDHR),[3] which contains dominant normative features of fundamental rights, followed by the International Covenant on Economic, Social and Cultural Rights (ICESCR).[4] The definition of socio-economic rights does not, however, stand alone. They are often placed in juxtaposition with civil and political rights, which in turn are revealed in the International Covenant on Civil and Political

---

2 Henry J. Steiner, Philip Alston, *International Human Rights in Context. Law, Politics, Morals*, Oxford University Press, 2000, p.242-245.

3 Universal Declaration of Human Rights, adopted and proclaimed 10 December 1948, G.A. Res.217 A (III).

4 International Covenant on Economic, Social and Cultural Rights, adopted 16 December 1966, G.A. Res. 2200A (XXI), 1 UN GAOR Supp. No. 16, UN Doc. A/6316 (1966); entered into force 3 Jan. 1976 [hereinafter ICESCR]. Note that for the purposes of this study the part of the Covenant concerning cultural rights will be omitted, assuming therefore that whenever a reference to the Covenant is being made, the author has social and economic rights in mind.

Rights (ICCPR).[5] Along the legal scholarly debate a certain tension arises when the interrelation between socio-economic and civil and political rights is being discussed. It is claimed that the dichotomy between *social and economic* and *civil and political* rights stems from their categorisation into two legal categories of human rights and from their textual formulation within separate international treaties.[6] The scientifically oriented research has usually been concerned with civil and political rights, assigning them priority to social and economic rights and confronting the two on the basis of positive-negative connotations.[7] It is obvious, however, that they both constitute undeniable pillars of the fundamental and universal human rights.[8] The difficulty in dealing with legal categorisation of human rights has shifted onto national level, where the clash between both categories of rights is well reflected in constitutional debates, be it either over already existing constitutional provisions or where new constitutional bills are drafted. An ongoing debate is reflected within the scope of welfare rights, their modes of materialisation and methods of effective implementation. However,

---

5 International Covenant on Civil and Political Rights, adopted 16 December 1966, G.A. Res. 2200A (XXI), 1 UN GAOR Supp. No. 16, UN Doc. A/6316 (1966), entered into force 23 March 1976 [hereinafter ICCPR].

6 *Civil and political rights* and *social and economic rights* as two separate categories of rights are often referred to as respectively first and second generation human rights. This division reflects a historically grounded chronology of the importance assigned to each set of rights.

7 Such an approach is highly contested by number of scholars, who point out the artificiality of the division between positive-civil and political rights and negative-social and economic rights. Some civil and political rights may require a positive state action; for this argument see: Cécile Fabre, *Constitutionalising Social Rights*, 6 Journal of Political Philosophy, 1998, p. 268-270.; while some social and economic rights may demand state non-interference with individual action; for this argument see: Henry Shue, *Basic Rights: Subsistence, Affluence and US Foreign Policy,* Princeton University Press, 1980 p. 39-40, 55-56. In general see: Wojciech Sadurski, *Constitutional Courts in the Process of Articulating Constitutional Rights in the Post-Communist States of Central and Eastern Europe. Part I: Social and Economic Rights*, EUI Working Paper LAW No. 2002/14 2002.

8 Although interesting, the debate over the reasons for a clear distinction between social and economic and civil and political rights at the UN level has to be set aside for the sake of the consistency of argument. Suffice to say, that the categorisation of fundamental rights resulted from a certain aspiration towards the formalism of human nature, which is reflected in an attempt to develop a shared sense of understanding of given human rights- of their substance and context and of their application. Certainly, this aspiration was embedded in antagonisms between democratic and communist regimes of the époque. An attitude towards the universal legal formulations of rights and presumptive resulting categories of these rights is indeed a characteristic feature for international debates, where the clashes of cultures and political interests meet.

the growing importance of socio-economic rights and the awareness of constitutional scholars requires a more efficient formulation of social and economic rights within the constitutions.[9]

Yet, it is claimed by some scholars that the particular nature of social and economic rights, despite their universal definition in the international treaties such as ICESR, results from the need for contextual understanding.[10] This claim highlights the problem of the relative assignment of these rights in a specific community or state. One may expect, therefore, that there is a need to extract a comprehensive set of social and economic rights for research purposes depending on the angle and scope of the conducted study.[11] In these lines several attempts were made in order to identify core social and economic rights as basic for human welfare and survival through an attempt to create an index capturing the substance of the chosen social and economic rights.[12] Finally, not only the context but the scope remains disputed. Some scholars define socio-economic rights as "subsistence rights" (such as the right to adequate food, clothing, shelter, unpolluted water and basic healthcare), others claim that the core social and economic rights are welfare rights, since they reflect the most basic and universal values.[13]

Before dealing with the specificity of constitutional social and economic rights, the three focal points for the discussion on the nature of social and economic rights will be presented. The concept of social and economic rights will

9 This general argument will be further developed in the context of debates over social and economic rights' constitutionalisation in the 1990s in Poland, the Czech Republic and Slovakia.

10 In the argument against the inclusion of social and economic rights in Eastern European constitutions, Sunstein argues that constitutions must be compatible with the culture and mores of those whom they regulate. The author implies that this is a specific situation of transition from communism to market economy which hampers constitutionalisation of social and economic rights. See: Cass R. Sunstein, *Against Positive Rights*, 2 East Europ. Const. Rev., 1993.

11 See: Clair Apodaca, *Measuring Women's Economic and Social Rights Achievement*, 20 Hum. Rts. Quarterly, 1998.

12 Henry Shue, *op.cit.*, p. 22-29. By tracing back subsistence rights to *minimal economic security*, Shue claims that the former, can be well justified for treatment as a basic right on the same reasons as physical security, which in turn is usually less controversial than the justification of subsistence rights.

13 William E. Forbath, *Constitutional Welfare Rights. A History, Critique and Reconstruction*, 69 Fordham L. Rev., 2000-2001; Frank I. Michelman, *The Constitution, Social Rights, and Liberal Political Justification*, 1 Int. Journal Constitutional Law, 2003.

be briefly introduced as a theoretical background to this category of rights, and will be further divided into four arguments: legal, political, economic, and moral, which therefore constitute principal issues in arguments in favour of or against constitutional justiciability of social and economic rights. Furthermore, a distinction between the material and procedural nature of social and economic rights will be suggested, which is intended to serve for further argumentation on the differentiated nature of the very social and economic rights; that is the distinction of the enforceability of rights is done within the socio-economic rights themselves.

This means that, on the one hand, there are some social and economic rights which are directly enforceable by a constitution (even though some of them are subject to a clause which explicitly delegates the duty to determine the scope and form of their implementation to the legislature), yet, on the other hand, there are some which are conditioned by a legislative discretion. First, however, the concept of social and economic rights within a wider philosophical setting will be introduced.

1.1.1 Scope of Socio-Economic Rights

When discussing the nature and scope of social and economic rights, a distinction between the meaning of *rights*, *needs* and *preferences* must be established to begin with. This pivotal but difficult distinction reflects doubts and divisions that question the legal enforcement or/and constitutionalisation of social and economic rights present in different political, cultural and socio-economical regimes. It is crucial to note that first, the ordinary *needs* are different from the *social needs*.[14] By posing moral questions in the process of simple redistribution in a non-ideal society, *social needs* result from different prerequisites than *individual needs*. The latter is concentrated on the ego-centric vision of an individual and thus should be named as *preferences* or *wants*. This is not however to say that social and economic rights are attributed to a society rather than to an individual. The idea that individuals provide the basis for law and society is based on the purpose of an organized civil society, which is to further the ends of individuals. In this context social and economic rights provide each and every

---

14 There are four main categories of a need : a normative need (identified according to a norm, or set standard), a comparative need (reveals problems which emerge by comparison with others who are not in need), a felt need (the one felt by an individual), and finally an expressed need (an articulated or unarticulated need). The famous Bradshaw's classifications of social needs cited after: Nick Manning, *Social Needs, Social Problems and Social Welfare*, in: Pete Alcocl et al. (eds.), *The Student's Companion to Social Policy*, 2003.

individual with the fundamental necessities to fulfil such rights for example the right to education. Attribution of social rights to an individual empowers the society with the tools to realise the social needs. And while the satisfaction of *social needs* is a means of "breaking the cycle of discrimination", it proves the compatibility of socio-economic rights with the principle of equal treatment.[15] Moreover, the focus of the *social need* as a condition to ensure social and economic rights, reflects the logic of the fulfilment of a further function, purpose and / or end of a given right.[16] This being said, these rights are sometimes taken as: "legitimate social, economic, and cultural needs of individuals and groups of individuals".[17]

As noted before, when discussing the genesis of social and economic rights the case of the normative interdependence of these rights with civil and political rights is often evoked by scholars.[18] Yet another interesting dimension of the nature of social and economic rights relates to their "internal" categorisation. May social and economic rights be considered as two separate components, *the social* and *the economic* rights? Such a distinction may seem to be dubious in a sense that it introduces exclusive social and economic components of each right. It would therefore mean that social rights inherently exclude the economic com-

15 Further elaborated by Amy Gutman in the context of the satisfaction of the right distributive principle for employment. See: Amy Gutmann, *Justice across the Spheres*, in: David Miller & Michael Walzer (eds.), *Pluralism, Justice and Equality*, 1995, p.104-105.

16 The need to have food ("the right to food" as a subsistence right) would be a social need if it serves maintaining life and health, whereas the need of food understood as a fulfilment of desires for luxurious nutrition would not be a need but a wish or craving. For a more detailed distinction between needs and wants see inter alia: Anthony Flew, *Equality in Liberty and Justice*, Routledge, 1989, p.108-115.

17 Wiktor Osiatyński, *On Social and Economic Rights: A Needs-Based Approach,* Bulletin Transnational Center for Democratic Studies, *at* http://www.newschool.edu/centers/tcds/bulletinbackissues.htm.

18 For elaboration of the idea of interdependence of civil and political rights and economic, social and cultural rights see: C. Scott, *Reaching Beyond (Without Abandoning) the Category of "Economic, Social, and Cultural Rights"*, 21 Hum. Rts. Quarterly, 1999. The author claims for the two types of interdependence, pointing out a feature of one right actually being part of the other ("organic interdependence"; for example, the rights of infants to be protected from health threats that lead to infant mortality as a part of the right to life), or a situation where the two rights are distinct but one has a beneficial impact on the enjoyment of the other ("related interdependence"; for example, the rights to a fair trial can impact favourably on the right to social assistance).; for this see an earlier work of the same author: C. Scott, *The Interdependence and Permeability of Human Rights Norms: Towards a Partial Fusion of the International Covenants on Human Rights*, 27 Osgoode Hall L.J., 1989.

ponent and vice-versa. Nevertheless, modern social rights is accommodated by certain aspects of a neo-liberal economic logic.[19] Notions of contracts, competitiveness, and efficiency are widely used in the field of labour and social law. And, on the other hand, market relations are dependent on the notions of social rights, such as for example an idea of equal access to economic resources. There is a reason, however, for which some rights are more "social" and some are more "economic". The right to an adequate standard of living, usually taken as a core *social* right, affects primarily these parts of a population, which are on the bottom of the socio-economic hierarchy.[20] By concentrating on the most deprived groups, social and economic rights are more direct in addressing the problem of reducing poverty. Social welfare enhances the principle of well-being of each and every individual and of the society as a whole. It reduces societal differences and thus, diminishes the risk of possible social tensions. Also other traditional social rights –like a right to health care, education,[21] or social security- pertain to the needs not only of the economically marginalised but to the whole society.[22] These rights contribute to the building of stable social structures and thus, encourage the influence of the civil society through shifting the responsibility of providing welfare from the competences of the state to the capacity of the organized structures of the civil society. On the other hand, it is claimed that in some of the rights the economic character is dominant due to the orientation and reciprocal relationship of the right and the economic factors. For example the right to work[23] -and more specifically to favourable conditions of work, or a guarantee of a minimum wage necessary for a decent living- the right to property,[24] the right to social security,[25] rights to form and advocate through

---

19 Simon Deakin, *Social Rights in a Globalized Economy*, in: Philip Alston (ed.), *Labour Rights as Human Rights*, 2005, p.52.

20 UDHR, Art.25; ICESCR, Art.11; ICRC, Art.27.

21 The right to education is sometimes considered as a cultural right. The bearing of this upon its societal consequences, and for the purpose of this study it will be regarded as a social right. In the contribution to a person's well-being the right to free education is a social good, in its aspect of the contribution to enhancing participatory behaviour it is, however, considered as a political right, and consequently a political duty. Education does not only facilitate life chances and participation in other citizenship activities (voting, or seeking redress through the courts) of an individual. It raises a general standard of living in a given society and influences other aspects of welfare provision like health, social security, and employment.

22 Henry J. Steiner, *Social Rights and Economic Development: Converging Discourses?*, 4 Buffalo Hum. Rts. L. Rev., 1998, p.28.

23 UDHR, Art.23; ICESCR, Art.6.

24 UDHR, Art.17.

25 UDHR, Arts.22, 25; ICESCR, Art.9; ICRC, Art.26.

trade unions[26]- they all require financial resources but also stimulate economic development.

It follows from the above that social and economic rights are supplementary, and interrelated. One right is a consequence of the other and they entail the "surrounding right". A sharp distinction between what constitutes a social and what constitutes an economic right is hard to draw. Moreover, the spill-over-effect triggers an interaction of socio-economic and civil and political rights. The affirmation of uniformity of all rights stems from a principle laid down in the Final Declaration of the Vienna World Conference on Human Rights of 1993 that "all human rights are universal, indivisible, interdependent and interrelated".[27] All things considered, both civil and political, and social and economic rights have to be treated in an equal manner. The question of possible tensions between rights does not therefore concern the substantive sphere of social and economic rights but it touches upon the actual enforcement and materialisation of these rights in concrete public policies.

In conclusion, the above arguments entail two characteristics that depict the relationship between social and economic, and civil and political rights: it is a non-exclusive and category-crossing relationship. Otherwise, the ultimate goal of ensuring respect for the dignity of an individual cannot be achieved, since the dignity of an individual is only assured when a person enjoys all of his/her rights. [28] It must be noted that in principle everyone should be a beneficiary of human rights.[29] In practice, however, the application of social and economic rights encounters two substantive problems.[30] First, most obviously, concerns the differentiation of the degrees to which certain groups in the society require special protection of rights- some groups are more vulnerable than others, or traditionally have been subject to discrimination. Addressing inequalities in the society demands adoption of suitable measures, such as for example, the affirmative action. The second argument, a more basic one, relates to the funda-

26 ICESCR, Arts.6-8. Collective rights are not taken into account in this study. The rights which relate to trade unions and collective bargaining will be implicitly considered within a specific context, as the rights of associated individuals.

27 UN Doc. A/CONF.157/23, § I.5.

28 The concept emphasizing the indivisible, interdependent and interrelated character of all rights proves the efforts of the international community to underpin the integrity of all human rights. More on the grounding of social and economic rights in the constitutional principle of human dignity, will be elaborated further on in Chapter 2.

29 UDHR, Art. 22.

30 Asbjørn Eide, *Economic, Social and Cultural Rights as Human Rights*, in: Asbjørn Eide et al. (eds.), *Economic, Social and Cultural Rights*, 2001.

mental question of the duty-holder definition, which is usually restricted to the citizenry. The problem arises in respect to non-nationals (migrant workers, asylum-seekers, refugees, stateless), in relation to whom the consideration of the host state's responsibility may be difficult to determine, and consequently is then connected with the first concern presented above: the collective acceptance and readiness to enlarge the scope of the right's impact on an additional group of "strangers".[31]

1.1.2 Internal Components

In what follows, a closer look should be given to the distinctive elements of the content of social and economic rights. Namely, the relationship between the substantive (material) and procedural (non-material) dimension of these rights. From a technical point of view every right has its material substance and procedural transmission.[32] This dichotomy corresponds with the objective of rights convincingly formulated by Titmuss, who claimed that the objectives which shaped and influenced social security and social service programmes were the integration of all citizens into a society, and the stimulation of civil participation within the community.[33] Building on this theory, social and economic rights "facilitate access to benefits which the community has to offer and provide a base of material security below which the individual citizen may not fall", as well as "by extending participation rights from the public to private sphere they thereby ensure not only the social accountability of those who exercise private power, but also the right of individuals to participate in making of decisions which af-

---

31 The problem of identity and subsequent distinction between "an own group" and "strangers" has been widely discussed in the sociological discourse. It is assumed that the "we" – "they" distinction influences identity affiliation and by contrasting it with groups of strangers it builds different social borders, which in turn create new social divisions characteristic to a given society. The social divisions may be based on ethnicity, nationality, culture, religion, sex, age, but also on social aspects such as division between elites versus society, marginalisation on the grounds of poverty, education, etc.

32 For a discussion on the relationship between substantive and procedural rights see, e.g., Larry Alexander, *Are Procedural Rights Derivative Substantive Rights?*, Law and Philosophy, No. 17, 1998. Alexander examines a distinction between these two by pointing out that the procedural rights are substantive rights, albeit of a special kind: rights against risks. Discussing the substantive values with strong procedural implications, he refers to social entitlements, admitting that the point about procedural rights being derivative of substantive ones remains valid, although of a reduced significance.

33 Titmuss' deduction is based on a study of the relationship between social security programmes and social service benefits. For more details see: Richard M. Titmuss, *Commitment to Welfare*, Allen & Unwin., 1976.

fect them (...)".[34] It has to be clearly stated that this feature is revealed strictly for the argument which will be further developed in this study, and which concerns the change of substance between the understanding of social and economic rights in the Marxist and liberal doctrine.

Substantive or material dimension in the case of socio-economic rights may otherwise be referred to as claims to resources, through which the individuals are able to convert the commodities into potential or actual functioning. Therefore, the actual content is given to such rights like the right to social security, the right to health and education services, in a way that these rights, are transformed from the notion of "passive protection" into the one of "active security".[35] There is a close correlation of substantive socio-economic rights and the principles of equality of opportunity and social justice.[36] By serving the equality of opportunity, socio-economic rights are means which help to eliminate discrimination in terms of access to or participation in the civil society. They endure the access to education, training, and employment opportunities. By securing the removal of barriers- such as disability, religion or race discrimination- they facilitate participation of the individual in the civil society. Serving social justice, socio-economic rights guarantee that the basic needs of an individual, appropriate for the community in which they live, are ensured. At the same time, however, the shift from purely formal guarantees to the effective, judicially enforceable rights and policy initiative foundations must be followed by additional institutional preconditions, which allow the individual to participate and affect the shape of these rights and policy programmes in a way that these rights become suitably applicable to the individual. As previously mentioned, this is the concern of procedural or non-material rights to regulate the exercise of social power, protect the individual from the overbearing use of power, and facilitate participation in decisions taken by the delegated authorities who bear such power. The guarantees, which ensure the right to take part in forms of procedural or institutionalized interactions, touch upon "social or institutional settings that shape the set of possibilities open to individuals in terms of achieving their goals".[37]

---

34 K.D. Ewing, *op.cit.,* p.105.

35 S. Deakin, *op.cit.*, p.58-59.

36 K.D. Ewing, *op.cit.,* p.105-107.

37 S. Deakin, *op.cit.*, p.59.

1.2 Nature of Socio-Economic Rights

1.2.1 Legal Aspects

The legal argument in the debate on the nature of social and economic rights is first concerned with the problem of their justiciability and, consequently, with their judicial enforcement.[38] The question of justiciability of social and economic rights arises from the fact that these rights are often contrasted with civil and political rights. The discussion on the legal argument of the justiciability of social and economic rights is entrenched in the two opposing approaches to the issue. The first approach argues that socio-economic rights are inherently non-justiciable, and they cannot be judicially enforced. The juxtaposition of the traditionally considered as more vague social and economic rights and the precise civil and political rights leads to a dubious conclusion that regarding the issue of their nature only the latter rights may be decided in courts.[39] Moreover, social and economic rights are sometimes believed to be antagonistic, as they are expressed in such a way that they may involve violations of other rights (such as the case of a right to private education, which may generate unequal opportunities). Secondly, the materialisation of social and economic rights into social and economic policies is designated by some as an "anti-democratic process", since the functioning of legal institutions required for this purpose may be contestable.[40]

---

38 At this point a differentiation between the concept of justiciability and the concept of judicial enforcement is made. The justiciability of a right is understood as a right's general attribute that renders the right under the judicial process in which a judge can consider it in a concrete set of circumstances. This consideration can result in the further determination of the right's significance. The judicial enforcement, on the other hand, is explained as the actual consideration of the right within appropriate legal proceedings. The latter, therefore, entails the effects that the consideration of the right would bring. It would either take the form of a concrete judgement which adds itself to *acquis* of the national case law, or is embodied in constitutional review which reviews a law or an official act for the violation of basic principles of justice and depending upon the particular solution accepted by the system, may strike down the law, overturn the act, or confirm its conformity with the constitution.

39 Although social and economic rights as such are widely recognized, a problem arises with the recognition of their corresponding obligations. This ambiguity results from the fact that social and economic rights are formulated as broad obligations of results rather than specific obligations of conduct. For more see: Asbjørn Eide, *Realisation of Social and Economic Rights and the Minimum Threshold Approach*, 10 Hum. Rts. Law Jnl., 1989, p.36-38.

40 Michael Freeman, *Human Rights. An Interdisciplinary Approach*, Polity Press, Blackwell, 2002, p.165.

The principal objections to the justiciability of social and economic rights concentrate mainly around the conviction that the protection of social and economic rights lies within the competence of the legislature and executive and its constitutional protection would lead to an inevitable transfer of power from these two branches of government to the judiciary.[41] Claims are made that implementation of social and economic rights require making political choices, setting priorities, allocating resources and rearranging budgets.[42] These competences belong to the legislative and executive branches of the government. It is believed, consequently, that by adjudicating on social and economic matters courts infringe the principle of the separation of powers. Whereas, on the other hand, the opposite effect is reflected in the danger of the politisation of the courts, seen as a process of dragging the courts into a political bargaining process.[43] It is also believed that by the constitutional or ordinary judicial review of socio-economic rights, judges would be led to assess governmental social policies only on the basis of individual cases, which do not necessarily reflect the overall social situation in a given socio-economic environment. The lack of specific expertise among the judges to make complex decisions on social and economic issues, for example in the area of housing or health care, go hand in hand with an argument that in general courts lack the standards against which they could assess the performance of the government in socio-economic policies. Furthermore, judges are believed not to be competent enough to deal with social and economic cases, since they lack the democratic legitimacy necessary to make decisions on the allocation of social and economic resources. These are the representatives of legislature, and indirectly the representatives of the government, who have been democratically elected and given a mandate to decide on the social and economic policies. Adding to this, adjudication on technical, economic or budgetary areas again poses a problem of the responsibility limits among the three state power actors: executive, legislature and judiciary.

The negative argument against the stipulation of social and economic rights in the constitutions concentrates around the fact, already mentioned above, that social and economic rights are too general to be justiciable. The

41 For more see: Andreas Sajó, *How the Rule of Law Killed Hungarian Welfare Reform*, E. Eur. Const. Rev., 1996.

42 Fons Coomans, *Some Introductory Remarks on the Justiciability of Economic and Social Rights in a Comparative Context*, in: Fons Coomans (ed.), *Justiciability of Economic and Social Rights. Experiences from Domestic Systems*, 2006.

43 J. Cottrell, Y. Ghai, *The Role of Courts in the Protection of Economic, Social and Cultural Rights*, in: J. Cottrell, Y. Ghai (eds.), *Economic, Social and Cultural Rights in Practice*, 2004, p.86.

argument brought up by Sunstein, with reference to the comparison of Western and Soviet constitutions, is based on a conviction that to be justiciable, rights should be applicable only to the governments, and not to individuals, which implies a distinction between public and private spheres of rights' application. Since legal rights create legal duties and legal rights as such do not run against private persons, these are only states not individuals who are to be under constitutionally enforceable duties.[44] Moreover, the constitutionalisation of social and economic rights undermines the legal force of the constitution itself.[45] Especially in democratisation context, the inclusion of positive rights in the constitution may diminish the sense of entitlement to state protection and encourage individual initiatives, and second, these rights will not encourage positive changes accompanying the transition process. The latter argument is grounded in the concern that the role of constitutional courts may be that of policy makers, for which they are not qualified, thus, undermining the legitimacy of the constitutional court.[46]

On the other hand, however, there is no principled objection to justification of socio-economic rights, and thus their judicial enforcement. It is acknowledged that once constitutionalised, labour laws for example contribute to the more efficient protection of individual rights, as well as they encourage institutional guarantees in the form of imposing an obligation on the legislator to specify the constitutionally guaranteed rights.[47] It is no more difficult for a court, in addition, to determine whether an individual has received a fair remuneration than whether he or she has had a fair trial. In fact, civil and political rights have constrained the process of policy-making and resource allocation, so that the courts may no longer be blamed for the tendencies to usurp the policy prerogatives of the legislature and commanding governments on how to draw up the national budget.[48] A number of social and economic rights have proved to be enforceable in the context of domestic law.[49] Moreover, it is the national practice which shows that rights to social security may be heard in specialized courts; the industrial courts successfully deal with labour disputes, which to a considerable extent renders social and economic rights. It is thus practice rather than theory that allows the undermining of the arguments about courts' lack of capacity and legitimacy to adjudicate cases which relate to social and economic

44 Cass R. Sunstein, *Something Old, Something New*, East Europ. Const. Rev., No. 1, 1992.

45 Cass R. Sunstein, *Against Positive Rights, op. cit.*

46 Andreas Sajó, *op.cit.*

47 Marie-Ange Moreau, *Normes sociales, droit du traval et mondialisation. Confrontations et mutations*, Dalloz, 2006, p.239-240.

48 Malcolm Langford, *Judging Social Rights*, Human Rights Tribune, Vol.11, No.3, 2006.

49 The most creative and well-known case law comes from India and South Africa.

rights. As more and more practitioners indicate, social and economic concerns are brought to courts on a daily basis. The cases usually concern such problems as the disconnection from essential services, dismissals from employment and discrimination in schools.[50] It has to be admitted though, that the states' duty to take positive steps towards realisation of social and economic rights is more difficult for courts to adjudicate. Yet, this obligation is a legally binding obligation under Article 2(1) of the ICESCR, which requires that the states progressively realise these rights within maximum available resources. Furthermore, a number of governmental programmes have been launched by the state parties of the Covenant, which allows to believe that if the problem of adjudication on social and economic rights has not attained full attention, it is perhaps more a problem of mal-governance than the theoretical court's legitimacy to adjudicate and therefore protect and promote social and economic rights.

At this point the suitability of the distinction made between rights as both claims and needs, and principled goals of the state, proves to be relevant. The fact that these types of rights require different forms of judicial enforcement does not render them *ex definitione* unjusticiable. Moreover, it shall not be forgotten that the reinforcement of courts legitimacy and perhaps courts' compulsion to adjudicate on socio-economical cases comes from the activity and growing importance of the non-judicial bodies, as well as of the non-governmental, human rights organisations.[51] Yet, the problem of the lack of judicial legitimacy to deal with social and economic rights is rebutted by the argument that courts are usually reluctant to voluntarily enter into political debates, thus infringing the competences of the legislature and the executive. This reluctance stems form the fact that their performance is directed into their legitimate function, which is to watch over the performance of governments, bearing in mind the protection of the minority in the situation, where most democratic systems are based on majoritarian rule.[52]

50 Malcolm Langford, *Judicial Enforcement of Economic, Social and Cultural Rights*, Right to Food Journal, No. 2, 2003.

51 A more detailed research on the importance of the non-judicial bodies in promotion and protection of social and economic rights has been presented in Anna Maciejczyk, *Non-judicial system of socio-economic rights protection in Poland, the Czech Republic and Slovakia*, European University Institute unpublished 2007, (copy with the author).

52 Malcolm Langford, *Judicial Enforcement of Economic, Social and Cultural Rights, op. cit.*

1.2.2 Political Dimension

As all constitutional rights, the socio-economic rights are "translated"[53] into enforceable rights not only by courts, but also through law-making processes and various institutions. The legislature, the executive and the state administration play important role in implementation of constitutional socio-economic rights.

Like all constitutional rights, socio-economic rights are not only entrenched in a constitution, but are also protected as statutory entitlements in national legislations. By an enacted specific legislation the constitutionally defined norms are given effect, so that they are "translated" into a legislative act aiming at facilitating, providing and protecting access to the guaranteed basic resources. Such statutory measures encompass at one hand legislation which creates and empowers structures and institutions with more or less clearly defined mandate to protect and promote social and economic rights, and on the other the legislation which materializes the implementation of these rights. Statutory socio-economic rights take a traditional form of subjective legal entitlements of a particular person or a group of persons to particular benefits. The example being an entitlement to receive social assistance benefits if one meets certain eligibility criteria that can be enforced against the state. The parliaments are therefore the main legislative organs of social policies. They give a legal shape to national social policies; *ipso facto* by democratic procedures they determine the scope of state intervention in the domain of equalizing social chances and social differences of its citizens.[54] It is important to note in this place that the fact of "translation through legislation" of vaguely and generally phrased constitutional socio-economic norms enforces them in a way by giving them a more concrete and detailed substance. Moreover, such a "translated" norm is given a background, a certain justification coming from the higher norm. All things considered, one may expect that a statutory right is consequently more direct in the access to resources and enables its beneficiaries to assert one's rights. A specific "translation" of socio-economic rights and its conversion into policy programmes is done by the executive and state administration. Through the adoption of policies or through executive or administrative decisions, socio-economic rights are materialized and at the same time the respective institutions maintain a self-

53 Terms „translation through legislation" and "translation through executive and administrative actions" of socio-economic rights are used after Danie Brand. See: D. Brand, *Introduction to socio-economic rights in the South African Constitution*, in: D. Brand, C. Heyns, *Socio-Economic Rights in South Africa*, Pretoria University Law Press, PULP, 2005.

54 J. Auleytner, *Polityka społeczna, czyli ujarzmienie chaosu socjalnego*, Wydawnictwo Wyższej Szkoły Pedagogicznej TWP, Warszawa, 2002, p.319.

definition of the duties those rights impose on them. Thus policy formulation or administrative decision in a way "translate" constitutional rights into enforceable legal duties or entitlements. The judicial enforcement of these self-defined duties against the executive or administration is conducted by courts. On the other hand the existence of the non-judicial organs, such as ombudsmen, may lead to a remedial action taken in response to administrative malpractice. The latter inter-institutional mechanism has an indirect and consequently long-term effect, such as broader changes to administrative practice and general changes of the political and administrative culture.

Danie Brand presents an interesting depiction of the relationship between socio-economic rights defined through executive or administrative action on the one hand, and constitutional socio-economic rights on the other. According to Brand this relationship is of the same nature as a relationship between constitutional and statutory socio-economic rights.[55] First, once an executive or administrative action defines duties and entitlements in terms of constitutional socio-economic rights, it gives effect to these rights. In respect to its inherent nature, such right can be protected against challenge on other constitutional grounds. Furthermore, an executive and administrative materialization of constitutional socio-economic rights has to comply with the requirements of the right it is intended to give effect to.

The debate on social and economic rights often shifts from legal to political perspective, thus embodying the idea of welfare policy. Yet, again a vague understanding of social and economic rights, as it is often claimed, results in subordination of the socio-economic entitlements upon the development policies of the state, and also exposes the arbitrary political interest of parties and authorities in power. It is not clear how the problem of asserting rights to social protection within the framework of fundamental rights relates to the existing institutions of a welfare state, and to the patterns of actions or inactions by particular political actors- political parties, political leaders, ordinary courts, constitutional courts, state controlled organs, ombudsmen, etc. Especially interesting is the interaction between legislators and constitutional courts, which may lead to a phenomenon of "strategic behaviour". In such cases legislative would expose the political will to implement generous policy programmes, though being secured upon the constitutional review that, in most cases, does not implement costly solutions.[56]

55 Danie Brand, *Ibid*, p.17.

56 For a more detailed discussion see: Wojciech Sadurski, *Conclusions: On the Relevance of Institutions and the Centrality of Constitutions in the Post-communist Transitions*, in: Jan Zielonka (ed.), *Democratic Consolidation in Eastern Europe*, 2001.

1.2.3 Economic Reasons

The approach to the debate over justiciability of socio-economic rights in economic terms reveals the problem of the availability of resources required for the enforcement of these rights. The popular opinion revolves around the fact that it is meaningless to provide for rights without resource capacity to ensure their protection. The idea of the progressive achievement of socio-economic programmatic guidelines provides the reason for the enjoyment of these rights in reference to the availability of resources. It is of course contested by those who claim that the progressive achievement blurs the responsibility and allows the state only to arbitrarily justify its policies. Indeed, socio-economic entitlements are usually perceived only as instrumental to achieving certain ends- such as development and economic growth- and they are not even defined as rights but as aspirations or guidelines. However, it is not reasonable to believe that the lack of resources relieves the state of responsibility to provide for the well-being of the given society. The intrinsic value of social and economic rights is not debatable. Sen's "capability approach" proves the intrinsic value of social and economic rights, in a way that defines capability as "a kind of freedom: the substantive freedom to achieve alternative functioning combinations (…)."[57] While emphasizing the position of an individual with reference to the "realised functionings" (that is what a person is actually able to do), the notion encompasses at the same time the "capability set of alternatives" a person has; thus the real opportunities of individuals. Therefore, Sen argues that the enjoyment of socio-economic rights enhances the freedom of individuals by increasing their capabilities and quality of their life, and that the state is fully responsible for facilitating alternatives that the individual would be able to use.

Yet, another difference between the enforcement of the "negative" and "positive" becomes clear when the economic and financial aspects are taken into account. It is believed that civil and political rights can be immediately enforced since they require no intervention by the state, whereas social and economic rights require a positive action to be taken by state actors. This simplistic idea was refuted at the beginning (see above). The politics of the free market are confronted at this point with the political concepts which rely on the idea of state intervention. Needless to say, such relativism undermines the essential and fundamental characteristics of human rights, which is their irrefutable nature.

---

57 Amartya Sen, *Development as Freedom*, Oxford University Press, 1999, p.75.

1.2.4 Moral Justifications

The moral basis that favours the judicial enforcement of social and economic rights reflects the conviction that by virtue of being human, each individual has rights, and consequently, that by living in the community they have a moral claim to demand the right to live in dignity. One of the first sentences of the Preamble of ICESCR stipulates that the rights guaranteed in the treaty "derive from the inherent dignity of a human person". The UN Committee on Economic, Social and Cultural Rights (CESCR) widely debated the question of justiciability of social and economic rights. In the General Comment 9 on the domestic application of the Covenant, the Committee underlined the fact that despite variations in political systems, and while respecting competences of the various branches of government "courts are generally already involved in a considerable range of matters which have important resource implication. [Therefore,] the adoption of a rigid classification of economic, social and cultural rights which puts them, by definition, beyond the reach of the courts would thus be arbitrary and incompatible with the principle that the two sets of human rights are indivisible and interdependent".[58] The UN argumentation, with regard to its universal and global dimensions of reference should be considered rational, and proves that judicial enforcement in no way may be denied to economic, social and cultural rights on the grounds of their nature. It is rather "the lack of competence or willingness of the adjudicating body to entertain, examine and pronounce on claims affecting these rights".[59]

Yet, there is controversy around the moral claim for general justiciability of social and economic rights relating to the considerations on individual incentives and responsibilities for one's life. On this basis, it may seem dubious whether providing some groups and/or individuals with the goods and services enclosed in social benefits, is legitimate. The main reason is that there are unequal contributions from those better off to the benefit of those worse-off, but also those who only profit from the community welfare undermine the perception of social justice. There is no clear solution to this ambiguity. It is very difficult to demarcate a border line which would separate contributors from beneficiaries, especially in the individual-individual relations. Yet, in the realm of moral claims over social and economic rights, there will always be a degree of over-inclusion. Therefore, this issue should instead be considered as "a cost [which] has to be balanced against the costs of administering a highly individualized corrective justice".[60]

---

58 UN Doc. E/C.12/1998/24, § 10.

59 Office of the United Nations High Commissioner for Human Rights, *Economic, Social and Cultural Rights - Handbook for National Human Rights Institutions,* 2006, p.26.

60 Wojciech Sarurski, *Constitutional Courts in the Process of Articulating Constitutional Rights*..., p.39.

Chapter 2
Is There a Need for Socio-Economic Rights Constitutionalisation?

The extent to which social and economic rights are protected and enforced in a given society largely depends on the political culture and general awareness- both of the authorities and the society itself- for the need to grant and further fulfill these rights. At this point, the assumption is made that the relationship between the fulfilment of rights and their materialisation in the form of a given social policy programme does not only depend on their constitutionalisation.[61] This very general remark stems from the observation that the mere fact of constitutionalisation of socio-economic rights does not necessarily oblige the state to actively perform the role of a welfare state.[62] Moreover, a factor which deter-

61 The constitutionalisation of socio-economic rights varies across legal traditions and continuously brings forward the debate over the justiciability of these rights. In general, the European model is based on such principles as the one of the "Social State", which is mainly entrenched in the overall corpus of the constitutional legislation, even though a clear reference to it is not always the case. Almost all European countries are "social states" by the virtue of either explicitly adopted social state clause or by the direct enumeration of social rights in their constitutions. Unlike the European model, no constitutional foundation has been granted to the social policy in the U.S. For more see: G. S. Katrougalos, *The Implementation of Social Rights in Europe*, Colum. Jnl. European Law, 1996.

62 At this stage, an important terminological distinction between the terms "welfare state"(Wohlfahrtstaat, état-providence) and "social state" (Sozialstaat, État social) must be made. Despite their common interchangeable use, the two concepts are fundamentally different in nature. The idea of the welfare state was born in answer to the evolution of the functional necessities of the modern twentieth century capitalist economy, while the notion of the social state is related to a normative principle that constitutionalises governmental obligations in the field of social and economic policy. The social state, therefore, is a juridical form of organisation of a type of welfare state, which implies a guiding constitutional role for public power in economic and welfare matters in order to maintain social security and to minimize immense social differences. See: *ibid*, p. 277-278.

mines effective implementation and enforcement of socio-economic rights is the functioning of judicial mechanisms; an element which in fact is closely related to the question of how social and economic rights are incorporated into constitutions.[63] On the top of that, there is a definite interaction between autonomous social processes on the one hand and autonomous legal processes on the other hand, which are bridged by the constitution.[64] Since, the social processes and the legal processes are interdependent and they influence one another, it is important that the constitution provides for the framework for this double-track process; first, that it provides for the fundamental structures of the social system, which inform the law and is regulated by it; and second, that it formulates the basis on which the legal norms may be produced that are in turn interwoven with the fundamental structures of the social system. This having been stated, it must be noted that the two processes are defined differently by the constitution. The first takes the form of an explicit formulation of the legal basis in the shape of constitutional provisions, and provides for the institutional design of state power, while the second has a more substantive nature, and is embodied in the formulation of social and economic rights. This perspective imposes a twofold argumentation. The first argument relates to the sphere of social process of constitutional social and economic rights materialisation. It is reflected in the institutional framework within the constitutions which incorporate the question of institutional checks and balances between the executive and judicial authorities (understood here as the whole spectrum of legislative and executive state bodies versus constitutional courts). The second argument deals with the consequences of the functioning of an autonomous legal process, in a way that it leads to the explicit constitutional formulation of rights.

2.1 Are Socio-Economic Rights and Constitutions Compatible at All?

Given the diversity of historical legacies and the different character of constitutional provisions, the constitutional recognition of social and economic rights varies within each country to a considerable degree. After all, the constitution reflects the expectations of how a given community wishes to be governed. A constitution holds in the highest position among national legal acts and by the

63 See for example: Wiktor Osiatyński, *Rights in New Constitutions of East and Central Europe*, Colum. Hum. Rts. L. Rev., 1994, p.140.

64 Gunther Teubner, *Societal Constitutionalism. Alternatives to State-centered Constitutional Theory*, Ius et Lex, 27 May 2004.

holistic, though general expression of fundamental norms, it reflects the obligations of those who live in a given society, providing for a framework of implementation of these obligations in institutionalised social structures. Finally, it ensures fundamental principles, which both enable and disable the government to use its authority.[65] The constitution may thus contain both procedural and substantive rules, which by their nature are not neutral. Arguing, however, that in case of socio-economic provisions, this would predetermine the allocation of resources or redistribution of wealth, is an over-generalisation. Social and economic rights, understood as those that protect the dignity and the well-being of individuals, should be constitutionalised, since they indirectly limit the state power, putting an individual and his/her rights at the forefront of political concern.

Even when recognising that not all moral rights should be turned into legal rights, as their enforcement by the state may be impossible, there are some good reasons in accepting the challenge to introduce legal means by which individuals could be prevented from the violation of their fundamental rights. In case of socio-economic rights it would mean the guarantee of their materialisation either in the form of policy programmes, or as individual claims, to which states are under constitutionally enforceable duty. Such strengthening of these rights would protect them from being nominal only, as it was the case under communist constitutions. It has been ascertained moreover that transforming moral rights into legal rights imposes legal duties on individuals. This transformation is manifested through legal rights imposing legal duty on an individual not to harm the interests in which these rights are embedded - a feature also common to socio-economic rights.[66]

---

65 The argument of a constitution understood as pre-commitment strategies, brought up by Sunstein, arguing that the constitution should work against a nation's most threatening tendencies, veils the fundamental basis of this highest legal act at the domestic level, namely its legitimisation by the nation which it governs. This however, is not the most important counterargument in this place, as in certain cases "most threatening tendencies" of a nation should be frozen and denied at the constitutional level. These cases, however, relate to the situation when civil and political rights are misaligned with their proper content, as for example infringements of the right to life, or freedom of speech. On the contrary, social and economic rights, especially those falling under the category of subsistence rights, should be enforced by the constitution, taking into account its vague nature.

66 C. Fabre, *op.cit.*, p.100.

2.2 Justiciability of Constitutional Rights and Constitutional Duties

The justiciability of both constitutional rights, but even more so, of constitutional duties in the field of social and economic rights is widely questioned, mainly amounting to the problem of a lack of capability of constitutional courts to make decisions about the implementation of these rights (see the arguments discussed in the previous chapter). In general, the justiciability may vary according to four main factors: the characteristics of the case, the wording of the provision that is invoked, the attitude of the judge, and the general characteristics of the domestic system.[67]

Describing social and economic rights on the statutory level implies that they are regarded as legitimate provisions for the regulation of resources redistribution and they may define choices between competing values. By the same token, they are placed under political not judicial considerations. Furthermore, the statutory dimension provides social and economic rights with a less absolute character as opposed to the constitutional formulation. This is because a statute can be more easily changed than the constitution. Consequently, the undeniable and unconditional protection of all of the rights is ensured by their constitutional status.[68] A common distinction between constitutional provisions juxtaposes constitutional social and economic rights and constitutional social and economic duties. This distinction also discerns between the enforceable constitutional claim and the constitutional provisions (guiding principles or "programmatic rights"),[69] which set a state's policy goals within the field of social and eco-

67 F. Coomans, *op.cit.*, p.4 and also F. Viljoen, *National Legislation as a Source of Justiciable Socio-economic Rights*, Social Economic Rights Review, No.6, 2005, p.6.

68 Yet the issue of states' obligations under international human rights law may not be forgotten at this point of the discussion. By virtue of being a party to the ICESCR a state is required to give it a legal effect in the domestic order. Even if the rights resultant from the Covenant are not incorporated into domestic law, any state party must be considered as having accepted the rights provided for therein as subject to effective remedies. Therefore, any downgrading of social and economic rights in domestic policy programmes is clearly incompatible with the ICESCR. From this it follows that whether or not the constitution provides for the protection of social and economic rights, and when confronted with these rights, courts must aim to achieve the interpretations of domestic law which conforms with the recognition of social and economic rights recognised by the Covenant as rights rather than policy goals.

69 W. Sadurski, *Constitutional Courts in the Process of Articulating Constitutional Rights*... p.39.

nomic policy. In the latter, a state is expected to create conditions and mechanisms which enable the fulfilment of a given right.

The issue of another categorisation of the socio-economic rights, at constitutional level, was widely discussed and argued among scholars. Some claim, that with respect to the inherent nature of these rights, they have to be considered as equally valued provisions, and any hierarchy among them inevitably leads to the negation of the intrinsic value of the social and economic rights. Others point to doubts in enforcing rights considered as entitlements, which provide for paternalistic solutions. Nonetheless, the constitutional practice proves there is an answer to this question. A number of national constitutions distinguishes between constitutionally enforceable and non-enforceable social and economic rights.[70] Yet, again this fact does not disapprove the constitutional justiciability of these rights. However, this categorisation is not clear and the question asked at this point does not concern constitutional justiciability. Instead it relates to constitutional enforcement and the judicial mechanism adopted for this purposes. What needs to be recognized is that different judicial procedures result in different outcomes.

The debates between legal, political, economic or moral arguments have revealed diverging approaches to the justiciability of social and economic rights in general. Yet, the question which is being addressed here concerns the dimension of the judicial enforcement of the constitutional provisions. It is considered that once constitutionalised social and economic rights are justiciable, the problem of the consequences of their materialisation arises. Some of the rights will certainly be considered as claim rights, belonging to an individual's inherit entitlement to live in dignity. The others, stay within the realm of a state's competences and within the reality of a state's capacity or intention to shape the welfare policy. It has to be stressed at this point that this approach does not amount to the cate-

70 As for the distinction between constitutional enforceable and non-enforceable social and economic rights within a comparative constitutional perspective, the categorisation is complex. A classic example of the constitution which makes social and economic rights equally enforceable as civil and political rights is the constitution of the Republic of South Africa. Italian and Hungarian constitutions regard social and economic rights on an equal footing with civil and political rights, which implies that they are either identically enforceable or not. Chapters on social and economic goals are enshrined in the constitutions of Spain and Portugal, while directive principles in reference to these rights are present in the Indian constitution. Germany's constitution has only a general clause that is used to determine social and welfare policies on a statutory level. Yet, in the French and Swedish constitutions it is only the preamble that mentions the social goals of the state, thus rendering these rights into the category of constitutional duties.

gorisation of socio-economic rights by arranging them into any hierarchical line. It shows and acknowledges a wide constitutional practice that recognizes and enforces constitutional social and economic rights on different levels. However, the issue of implementation of the guiding provisions remains unsolved. The difficulty in this respect is caused by the imposition of the distinction between the protection of, for example, an individual's right to health care and the goal of health promotion by state authorities. All things considered, there will always be an overlap between these measures taken to reach a goal in a given social policy area and those which ensure the protection of the rights of individuals or groups of individuals. The capabilities of the state in the performance of its international obligations under the ICESCR or any other regional or international instrument, which envisages the protection and promotion of social and economic rights, has to be seen as the greatest possible effort to ensure the basic minimum of social and economic rights. The state cannot consider the ability condition, indeed a softening provision of the binding socio-economic obligations, as an excuse or justification of a malpractice or non-action in the sphere of social and economic policies. This is why, state actors such as constitutional courts, or national non-judicial bodies play an important role in the safeguarding of states' fundamental obligations. In light of this, the rights which fall into the category of directive principles and which define state's obligations in welfare policies must be considered as binding.

Taking into account the differences between legal protection of rights and political process of formulation and enactment of public social and economic policies, there are two aspects which need to be considered. The first concerns differences between the functions of the two categories of rights, namely the ones that are judicially enforceable and the second, those which are considered as programmatic goals. This approach consequently brings about questions over the effectiveness of the direct provisions of services provided for by a state with regard to the nature of a given right. Some of the rights provide for limitations to the power of the state, or have a procedural function which encourages individuals to participate in the life of the society. Yet, there are rights, which once guaranteed, require the state to ensure the entitlement to the direct provision of goods and services to the holders of rights. The characterisation of socio-economic constitutional provisions as vague norms does not necessarily question their justiciability. Actually, this argument is very often evoked in a general claim that all constitutional provisions, no matter whether civil and political or social and economic, are by their nature vague. Such an attempt questions the justiciability of the constitution as entire legal act. For the sake of argument at this point, it is assumed that the legal force of the constitution in itself may not be undermined, if the constitution is to be treated as a legitimate source of domestic law. Secondly, as shown in the argumentation above, the distinction between civil and political and social and economic rights may not be considered as mutually exclusive of, contradictory to or conflicting with rights. Recognising them as mutually enforceable, intra-related and supplementary encapsulates the fragility of the recognition of human rights as fundamental rights of individuals.[71]

Yet again, constitutionally protected social and economic rights are not all the same, since their judicial enforcement requires the adoption of different mechanisms. On the one hand there are mechanisms which allow an individual or groups of individuals to claim his/her/their rights, on the other hand there are mechanisms that ensure the checks-and-balances between state powers in terms of the proper fulfilment of a state's obligations within the field of the realisation of social and economic rights with respect to the international obligations and domestic obligations towards its citizens.[72] Although, there is no particular reason to claim that social and economic rights should not have a horizontal and vertical effect at the same time, meaning that they could be enforced both against individuals and against the state where appropriate, it remains impossible to imagine that the duty of a state could be enforced by one private party against another.[73]

The next division of categories of social rights concerns their status within the legal system. The distinction between constitutional and ordinary social rights will most probably not offend our conventional wisdom. Constitutional social rights are mostly discussed by scholars and practitioners with regard to their specific nature. The same is not true with respect to social rights defined at the ordinary law level. There seems to be a consensus in the understanding of social rights provided for by ordinary legislation as rights that do not bring legal disputes as to their nature, but rather that bring questions and doubts on the legal reality they shape. The question here is whether these rights are compatible within the system, whether they create a comprehensible system of social protection, and whether or not they are empty rights.

---

71 For the distinction between human rights and fundamental rights see: Gianluigi Palombella, *From human rights to fundamental rights*, EUI Working Paper LAW No. 2006/34, 2006. For the purposes of this book no distinction between the meanings of the above terms will be made.

72 As noted above, the aspect of application of social and economic rights to the citizens or non-citizens has only been signalled and will not be studied in depth.

73 K.D. Ewing, *op.cit.*, p.121.

The doubts described above are reflected in the constitutional transformation of socio-economic rights within the processes of democratisation. The crux of the matter in the reformulation of social rights within the post-communist constitutions was the determination of state duties in the materialisation of these rights. The Polish case serves as a good example. In general, Polish constitutional doctrine recognised social rights formulated in the 1997 Constitution as positive rights, understood as the domain of a state's obligation to undertake actions. Consequently, the function of the state in enforcement of social constitutional rights implies an obligation to act on the one hand, and on the other it creates expectations and claims from individuals towards the state to specific benefits and services. The duty of the state is to undertake activities that aim at enabling the entitled individuals to obtain pensions, and other social benefits, to get a place in a public school or in a public hospital.[74] This approach shows that the role of the state in formulating social policies is no longer considered an injunction to interference within the sphere of individual freedoms. This argument opens up a debate over the extent of democratic decision-making in enforcing constitutional social rights. The controversy revolves around two diverging opinions: whether the constitution specifies duties in a way that they are inseparably grounded in social rights,[75] or whether it leaves some scope for democratic decision-making. On the one hand, it is believed that the nature of social rights places duties on the state to provide people with the resources they need. On the other hand, it is claimed that these rights provide for a limited, responsive and accountable government.[76] Yet, at the same time social rights are also understood as the type of rights that do not require the state to "give" but instead to "create". In this regard, social rights enable its addressees to undertake actions

74 Leszek Garlicki, *Polskie prawo konstytucyjne. Zarys wykładu,* Warszawa, 2006, p.88.

75 Wojciech Sadurski, *Postcommunist Charters of Rights in Europe and the U.S. Bill of Rights*, Law and Contemporary Problems, Vol. 65, No.2, 2002, pp. 223-250; Wiktor Osiatyński, *On Social and Economic Rights: A Needs-Based Approach*, Bulletin of Transnational Center for Democratic Studies, Vo. 13/3, No. 45, 2003; Jerzy Ciemniewski, *Konstytucja państwa socjalnego czy liberalnego?,* in: Prawo w okresie przemian ustrojowych w Polsce, Warszawa 1995. Sadurski for instance claims that social rights should not belong to constitutional bills of rights, since by nature they contrast with aims of the constitution, which serves to limit state's powers rather than enlarge them.

76 Roman Wieruszewski, *National Implementation of Human Rights*, in: A. Rosas, I. Helgesen (eds.), *Human Rights in a Changing East/West Perspective,* London, 1990. Yet, it may be argued that since constitutional social rights are „surrounded" by procedural and institutional provisions that characterise democratic legislative processes, it provides a scope for a constitutional dialogue between the legislature and the Constitutional Tribunal. (The latter is the author's suggestion, supported by the study of the Constitutional Tribunal jurisprudence).

that allow them to develop proper rights within the system that the state creates. Here, the principle of solidarity is important, as it has a significant meaning for the fulfilment of constitutional social rights.

2.3 Characteristic of Constitutional Social Rights and Freedoms – post-transitional example

In seeking to define constitutional social rights some general remarks from the Polish constitutional doctrine are chosen to address the specifics, if any of post-transitional socio-economic rights. A preliminary distinction is drawn in the Constitution itself. Namely, most current constitutional formulation introduces two concepts: those of rights and of freedoms. As often as these two terms are used in the literature, there is a confusion over what they refer to. In broad terms, the distinction is twofold. On the one hand it depicts two situations of individuals – subjects of rights and freedoms, and on the other it refers to a definition of the role of the state in guaranteeing the adequate rights and freedoms of individuals. An obvious observation at this place would not go further than stating that comprehension of the two concepts varies across the legal literature.[77] For the most part, it is the choice of the author to refer to one of these options, but it should be pointed out, that they are barely mentioned together. In brief, the freedoms versus rights distinction from the perspective of individuals means that on the one hand individuals have a freedom of action, which is not a derivative of a legal norm. On the other hand, individuals have a right to act or not to act according to the substance defined in a legal norm, or equally a right to expect other subjects of that norm to act or not to act according to the substance of that legal norm.[78] In turn, in the context of the role of the state, freedoms are defined as corresponding to situations in which the state has a duty not to interfere in the actions of individuals. Rights, accordingly, fit into a category of situations where the state has a duty to take action. Under the first model, freedoms take on the form of negative rights,

---

77 See: A. Łopatka, *Prawo człowieka- refleksje wokół pojęcia*, in: *Teoria prawa. Filozofia prawa. Współczesne prawo i prawoznawstwo*, Toruń, 1998, p.139; B. Banaszak, *Prawa człowieka i obywatela w nowej konstytucji Rzeczypospolitej Polskiej*, Przegląd Sejmowy, No. 5(22), 1997, p. 56; W. Sokolewicz, *Nowa rola konstytucji w postsocjalistycznych państwach Europy*, Państwo i Prawo, No. 10, 2000, p.25; L. Wiśniewski, *Prawo a wolność człowieka- pojęcie i konstrukcja prawna*, in: L Wiśniewski (ed.), *Podstawowe prawa jednostki i ich ochrona sądowa*, Warszawa 1997, p.55; also: B. Gronowska, in: Z. Witkowski (ed.), *Prawo Konstytucyjne*, Toruń 1998, p.87.

78 Jerzy Oniszczuk, *Wolności i prawa socjalne oraz orzecznictwo konstytucyjne*, Szkoła Główna Handlowa w Warszawie, Warszawa 2005, p.13.

while under the second model, rights draw upon positive obligations, and positive rights. Therefore, as far as the materialisation of rights requires the state to play an active role, then freedoms require an attitude of non-interference. Nevertheless, the problem becomes even more complex as non-interference does not imply inaction. Once the state undertakes an action it becomes difficult to assess the scope of its duties and responsibilities. But even more thorny is the issue of the anticipated claims of individuals towards the state, once it is judged that positive action has gone too far. The question is how to judge it, and how far such a judgement can limit a state's privilege to legislate.

2.3.1 Claim rights v. capability rights[79]

Separation of social rights together with economic and cultural rights from civil and political rights demonstrates the willingness to give them – in the strict sense – a specific meaning. Some understand social constitutional rights as rights that enable individuals to obtain necessary means for living and to satisfy basic material needs.[80] Nevertheless, this definition is opposed by those who believe that social constitutional rights serve as means to justify and generate claims towards the state.[81]

An elaborate opinion on the nature of constitutional social rights was given by one of the Polish constitutional scholars Wiktor Osiatyński.[82] Osiatyński points to the fact that social constitutional rights are claims to the concrete material content of a right, but not to a mechanism of realisation. In this respect, he refers to the distinction of individuals' rights in their strict sense, and deny justiciability of constitutional social principles, i.e. a right to demand the state to legislate in a concrete field of social policy. He refers to the justiciable character

79 The term *capability rights* is the author's. It is not used neither in the Polish legal literature nor Czech or Slovak. It introduced in the context of Derrida's circular reasoning over the concept of ability/right, which- based on the right to education- presupposes an access to the capacity or to instruction in order to gain access to this certain right. See: J. Derrida, *Privilege: Justificatory Title and Introductory Remarks*, in: J. Plug (trans.), *Who's Afraid of Philosophy? Right to Philosophy I*, Stanford University Press 2002, p.36-37.

80 P. Czarny, *Konstytucyjny status jednostki w państwie polskim*, in: P. Sarnecki (ed.), *Prawo konstytucyjne RP*, Warszawa 2002, p.110.

81 See: Speech of MP Jerzy Ciemniewski from 21 January 1993, during 35th seating of Sejm of the first cadence, day one, point one and two on the agenda. All speeches and interventions of MPs are available at Sejm's Web Site www.sejm.gov.pl.

82 Wiktor Osiatyński,*Wprowadzenie do praw człowieką*
http://www.hfhrpol.waw.pl/pliki/WOsiatynski_HistIFilo.pdf

of a right to education, a right to protection of health, a right to minimal social security benefits, and other social rights written into the constitution. Social rights, therefore, create a guarantee for the minimum economic security of an individual. This minimal economic security is set at a level which allows for the dignified claiming social rights. Social rights, according to Osiatyński, are different with respect to other rights, in the way that they entitle an individual to claim certain goods and services from the state, whereas other individuals gain the same goods and services on their own. This in turn, means that the execution of benefits of a certain value is the subjective matter of a claim, what implies that a claim is directed towards a society, which is obliged to guarantee certain minimal social security to an individual. Since society does not have a legal personality, as Osiatyński briefly explains, the state therefore repays its "debt". The state is then bound to undertake such actions (like redistribution of a national income), as would the enforcement of social rights allow for it. Redistribution is not however, the only means through which social rights' enforcement is feasible. A fundamental economic security is a defining feature of social rights, rather than equality of living standards. In these terms, the right to social security should not be understood as a right of social equality.[83] Accordingly, Osiatyński calls social rights "the rights through a state".[84] A state's responsibility for the well-being of its citizens is in fact the basis for the concept of social rights. Osiatyński in his analysis, explains the differences in the creation of the role of the state in enforcing civil and political rights on the one hand, and of social and economic rights on the other. Whereas, the role of the state in the enforcement of first generation rights amounts to the duty of the state to respect freedoms and develop rights, in the case of social and economic rights the role of the state's origins from its obligations, which only then generate a right of an individual to a concrete benefit or service.

2.3.2 Social rights as fundamental rights

There are at least three features that characterise fundamental rights, and which allow for reflection upon whether social rights fall into the category of fundamental rights.

The most basic attempt to define rights as fundamental is by claiming that their protection is considered essential by a given society. This idea supposes

83 Wiktor Osiatyński, *ibid.*, p.9.

84 This paraphrase is contrasted to another one representative to the development of the social rights doctrine, namely "freedom from the State".

that fundamental rights form the core of rights; they play a pivotal role in a society and they constitute an objective which orientates institutions and policies.[85] The constitutional formulation of rights, also of social rights, should naturally be the most obvious evidence for attributing those rights fundamental character. Notwithstanding, however, the fact that the constitutional recognition of social rights is desired in order to consider them fundamental, the recognition of their enforceability and implementation mechanisms is a critical point in such a conceptual embrace. Hence the question is not so much whether constitutionalisation of social rights makes them fundamental, or rather confirms their essential attribute. The mere constitutionalisation does not make any rights fundamental.[86] It is important therefore, that fundamental (constitutional) rights are supported by adequate mechanisms of implementation and protection. The materialisation of these rights is only guaranteed when there are institutional and procedural instruments, which enable their realisation. Indeed, this was the crux of the matter discussed during the constitutional debates in Poland. The controversy came with both the reformulation of existing constitutional social rights under the 1952 Constitution, and with embracing them in a democratic institutional context that would guarantee their enforcement and promotion.

Yet, crucially, the understanding of social rights as fundamental rights is discussed in the literature within the framework of a more legal issue, namely the interdependence of rights and values. Osiatyński for instance, claims that human rights exclude certain values from the political process. Since human rights do not encompass all values or interests, they succeed in the event of collision with values or interests and therefore Osiatyński speaks about human rights as of fundamental rights.[87] With regard to values Wojciech Sadurski opposes this point of view, by claiming that in order to be fundamental, human rights need to be based on a set of political values and ideals, irreducible to the "rule-of-law" type values.[88] Although, Sadurski talks about individual liberty-

85 As Palombella suggests fundamental rights should be regarded within the context of the existence of a society, assuming that they are concretely implemented through the fabric of an organised social system; any change in the fundamental rights' model would result in a change of the societal model. See: Gianluigi Palombella, *From human rights to fundamental rights. Consequences of a conceptual distinction*, EUI Working Paper LAW No. 2006/34, 2006, p.3.

86 See: Anna Jaroń, *Constitutional Courts as Actors of Fundamentalisation of Social Rights,* EUI Working Paper Law No. 2009/05, 2009, p.9-10.

87 Wiktor Osiatyński, *op.cit.*, p.9.

88 Wojciech Sadurski, *Human Rights and Fundamental Values*, Archiv für Rechts-und Socialphilosohie, Beiheft 39, 1991, p.114-119.

rights, he defends his position in a principled manner. By and large, he resonates Mill's harm principle and Rawls' "priority of the right over the good" concept when it comes to shaping the content of law. He thus, believes that the state has to be neutral and may not interfere with individuals' preferences of what constitutes a morally good life for them, and consequently that the conceptions that define what gives value to human life exclude the principle of the independent content of law.[89] The issue is particularly relevant with respect to social constitutional rights, although it is perhaps harder to think of concrete conceptions that define the value of human life with respect to social rights, as social rights touch upon the core value of the human existence and to certain extents presuppose the content of law.

Insofar as the issue of fundamental (basic) rights are concerned, the judgements of 15 November 2000 (P12/99)[90] of the Polish Constitutional Tribunal are informative. It considers that in general constitutional rights arise from the principle of human dignity. From among these rights those that are fundamental are *ergo* natural, which refers directly back to human dignity and its essence. At the same time, in this judgement the Constitutional Tribunal stated that there are still further rights that need to be distinguished from fundamental (natural) rights. These are the rights that indirectly emanate from the human dignity principle and which merely constitute a form or one of the forms of the protection of human rights. The Constitutional Tribunal further ascertained that these rights enable the realisation of other rights and principles.[91]

Although often cited within the context of social rights, the role of the principle of human dignity was rarely commented upon in the Polish legal literature. It is equally true though, to observe that there are two fundamentally different opinions as to the use of this principle by the Constitutional Tribunal in cases concerning such issues as housing law, consumer protection, etc. Lately, a group of constitutional scholars criticised the use of the principle of human dignity as an interpretative guideline or the so called ornamental phrase in the cases concerning social rights. The leading constitutionalists claimed that: "[The principle of respect of human dignity] is not a universal remedy to all wrongdoings connected with the existence of a human being. Nor is it a new general clause applicable to an unlimited number of situations. It certainly cannot be used to regulate the social and economic system of the State or, more so, to rectify the gov-

89 Wojciech Sadurski, *ibid.*, p.114-115.

90 P 12/99, *Judgment of 15th November 2000* concerning principles of judicial control of decisions on extradition of foreigners from the Republic of Poland, published in: Dz.U. 2000.100.1085 of 21 November 2000. All judgements of the Constitutional Tribunal are published on Web Site www.trybunal.gov.pl.

91 See: Judgment P 12/99, p.15.

ernment's social policy".[92] Yet, this principle has also received recognition in one of the most recent, significant publications in the field, as an important element that plays a vital role in refocusing attention from the paternalistic protection of individuals from dangers coming from public structures and social groups, to rules that enable proper personal development within the framework of a society. Furthermore, it is assumed that the approach presented here, that is based on the "socialisation" of human dignity constitutes a modern standard in the protection of social rights.[93]

2.3.3 Enforceability of social rights

There are two counterbalancing opinions on the enforceability of constitutional social rights. Traditionally, the axis of the dispute divides scholars and practitioners for those who believe that social rights can be justiciable and for those who think that these rights, by their nature are not enforceable before the courts. The theory of course coincides with the practice, but it is often the case that scholars seem to forget about the diverging formulation of social rights that directly influences the extent of their enforceability. Some scholars claim that constitutional social (welfare) rights produce an "unfortunate institutional shift" in the separation of powers and, indeed, allow constitutional judges to enter into political discussions. On the top of that, the judges decide matters in which they have neither qualifications nor political authority.[94]

The institutional-competence argument was raised by a number of scholars in the early 1990s as a reaction to a proposal for a Social and Economic Charter, that was supposed to constitute one of the parts of the constitutional Bill of Rights in Poland.[95] The key point that was stressed in this respect, was that once a welfare right is constitutionalised, and even if subject to various provisions on

92 K. Działocha (ed.), *Basic Problems of Applying the Constitution of the Republic of Poland*, Sejm Publishing Office, Warsaw 2006, p.49.

93 Przemysław Mikłaszewicz, *Obowiązki informacyjne w umowach z udziałem konsumentów na tle prawa w Unii Europejskiej*, Wolters Kluwer business, Warszawa 2008, p.105.

94 Wojciech Sadurski, *Postcommunist Charters of Rights in Europe and the U.S. Bill of Rights*, Law and Contemporary Problems, Vol.65, No.2, pp.223-250, p.229.

95 Jerzy Ciemniewski, *Sejm i Senat w projekcie Konstytucji RP*, in: J. Krukowski (ed.), *Ocena projektu Konstytucji RP*, 1996, p.41-42; Wiktor Osiatyński, *Social and Economic Rights in a New Constitution of Poland*, in: A. Sajo, *Western Rights? Post-Communist application*, 1996 p.262-269; Andrzej Rapaczynski, *Constitutional Politics in Poland: A Report on the Constitutional Committee of the Polish Parliament*, in: A.E. Dick Howard, *Constitution Making in Eastern Europe*, 1993, p.107-108.

non-justiciability, there is nothing that will disable a constitutional court from scrutinising a government policy or a new law under the standard of the given constitutional provisions. By the same token, during discussions in Sejm in the 1990s, a doubt was expressed as to whether rights formulated as a policy guideline for the state can be enforced before the courts.[96]

As previously highlighted, apart from the catalogue of social rights and freedoms, constitutions also refer to the scope of the tasks and duties of the state that serves for the materialisation of the social rights of individuals.[97] It is claimed that without this reference to the system of the state's duties, nor without mechanisms that guarantee these rights, constitutional social rights could be regarded as declaratory only. The idea that defends this claim is an opposition to the redundancy of an ideological legacy of communism. The idea of an activist state protecting its citizens against economic downturns, together with the idea that citizens are entitled to a guaranteed standard of living, work, recreation and education, was compensated by the vision of a comprehensive system of policies that provide people with the opportunities to take care of themselves. Therefore, the ideology driven, empty constitutional rights, were supported by a system of courts and a democratically elected Parliament that was to ensure a proper realisation of state's obligations.

Again, however, programmatic norms bring in uncertainty as to the question of their justiciability and the coherence of the catalogue of social rights. It does not mean though that these are provisions of an ambivalent significance. The Polish Constitutional Tribunal for instance recognised in its numerous judgments that despite the fact that programmatic norms provide for general provisions, they have significant meaning in the creation and application of the law. Moreover, the lack of clear regulation in the constitution does not exclude state's obligation to positive action in the field of social policies.[98]

2.3.4 Limitations to social constitutional rights

The criterion which addresses the issue of legislative discretion and hence, determines means in which the state materialises social rights are the so called limiting clauses. Taking a closer look at Article 81 of the Polish Constitution helps to reveal the general functions of the limiting clauses.

96 See: Speech of MP Jerzy Ciemniewski from 21 January 1993.

97 B. Banaszak, *Prawo konstytucyjne*, Warszawa 2001, p.233.

98 J. Oniszczuk, *op.cit.*, p.38.

Article 81 of the 1997 Polish Constitution submits some of the social rights to the limits of the laws enacted to implement them. Submission of selected rights to the limits provided for by ordinary legislation entails two categories of rights: those which can be directly enforced with reference to the provisions of the constitution (and ordinary law provisions),[99] and those which can be enforced within the limits confined by laws.[100] The issue becomes even more complicated, since some of the articles, besides being limited by the Art.81 provision, have their own limitation clauses, which subject given rights to the ordinary laws. For example, the right to days free from work (Art.66.2) shall be specified by a statute, and may be asserted subject to limitations specified by a statute, as it arises from Art.81. What does this double limitation serve for? Does not it bring in, in fact, a differentiation between the "better" and the "worse" protected social rights?

The matter of a diverse enforceability of social rights enumerated in the Polish Constitution, was elaborated by the Constitutional Tribunal. In one of its judgements concerning the constitutionality of provisions regulating procedures of determination for the old-age pensions of those who served in the army, the Constitutional Tribunal's judgement SK 22/99 of 8 May 2000,[101] clearly stated that the two categories of social rights, stemming from application of Art.81, take effect with respect to the scope of the duties of the State. In this regard, while the content of the rights subject to the provision of the limitation clause are left to be decided by the legislator, the content of the remaining social rights is directly shaped by constitutional formulation, even if the constitution infers the formulation of concrete provisions to the ordinary legislation. In another judgment concerning the constitutionality of provisions that regulate procedures of assigning material help to stationary students only, judgment U 7/01,[102], the Tribunal went into detail in defining the groups of rights under

99 These are the following rights: right to ownership, other property rights and of succession (art.64), freedom to choose and pursue an occupation and to choose a place of work (art.51.1), prohibition of child labour (art.65.3), the right to social security in case of sickness, disability, old-age or unemployment (art.67), the right to health care (art.68), right to education (art.70), protection of rights of children (art.72), freedom of artistic creation and scientific research (art.73).

100 Art. 81 of the Polish Constitution relates to the following rights: right to a minimum wage (Art.65.4), right to full employment (Art.65.5), right to hygienic conditions of work and the right to days free from work (Art.66), aid to disabled persons provided for the public authorities (Art.69), protection of the family (Art.71), ecological security and protection of the environment (Art.74), right to housing (Art.75), and finally the protection of consumers and customers (Art.76).

101 SK 22/99, *Constitutional Tribunal Judgment of 8 May 2000*, published in: Dz.U. 2000.38.438 of 12 May 2000.

102 U 7/01, *Constitutional Tribunal Judgment of 2 July 2002*, published in: Dz.U. 2002.104.933 of 11 July 2002.

diverse enforceability. Here, three groups of rights were referred to, depending upon the scope of legislative discretion. In the first place, the Constitution refers to provisions where policy goals and strategies are indicated. Such a formulation, according to the Tribunal, does not entail the state's duty to materialise these goals through ordinary legislation.[103] Next, there is a group of rights that is subject to the state's obligation to materialise them through acts of laws.[104] And finally, with reference to the third group of rights, the constitution indicates the duty to legislate and it also defines the substance or direction of a specific regulation.[105] Although explicitly discussed in the constitutional jurisprudence, it seems obvious that the identification of a pedigree of legislative discretion is hard to define in practice.[106] Importantly, this entails two other aspects subject to the critique of the impracticability of constitutionalisation of social rights. Firstly, it is assessed that the delegation of the regulation of detailed constitutional rights and benefits by the ordinary legislator is a weak point of the Constitution.[107] Moreover, it remains unclear whether the legislative discretion in this field is full, or whether there are some standards that the legislator needs to obey in shaping social policy elements.[108]

As already mentioned in the judgement P 12/99, within the context of constitutional scrutiny of the principle of the openness of the trial (Art.45.1 of the Constitution), the Constitutional Tribunal referred to the principle of human dignity and established a limitation to those rights that do not directly emanate from it, but rather enable the realisation of other (here: fundamental) rights. In the view of the Tribunal the latter, unlike the fundamental rights, can be "shaped" within the framework of axiology of the *democratic state ruled by law*.[109] Though, it is not a straightfor-

---

103 Here the Tribunal enumerates the following articles: 65.5, 68.3, 68.4, 68.5, 69, 72.1, 72.2, 74.1, 74.2, 74.4, 75.1.

104 Rights in the following articles fall into this category: 66.1, 67.1, 67.2, 68.2, 69, 70.4, 71. 2, 76 sentence 2.

105 This applies to articles: 64.3, 65.1-4, 66.2, 70.1, 70.3, 75.2.

106 Short of comprehensive enumeration, the Tribunal explicitly stated in the same U 7/01 judgment and repeated it in numerous other decisions concerning social rights, that whether beneficiaries of public authorities' actions defined in the three groups of rights are eligible to claim concrete actions from the authorities, is a matter of a separate, case-by-case analysis that should be performed by the Constitutional Tribunal. See in: U 7/01, *Constitutional Tribunal Judgment of 2 July 2002*, p.9.

107 B. Banaszak, *op.cit.*, p.233, also: K. Działocha (ed.), *Basic Problems of Applying the Constitution…*, p.59. Here the report suggests that the *ad casum* reading of the Constitution in social matters means that deciding specific disputes about the relevant differentiation criterion may be regarded as unsatisfactory in view of the lack of broad substantive argumentation.

108 J. Oniszczuk, *op.cit.*, p.41-42.

109 P 12/99, *Judgment of 15th November 2000,* p.15.

ward juxtaposition of civil and political versus social and economic rights. In this judgment the Tribunal indicates that not all of the rights have the same absolute "power" with respect to the limits that may be put upon them by ordinary legislation. By dealing with the issue of limitations that the legislator may confer upon constitutional rights, the Tribunal clearly states that there are two conditions that: firstly, mean that the Constitution itself or by the way of a reference to the ordinary legislation envisages, and secondly, that the concrete limitation is acceptable taking into account the nature of a right. Moreover, the Tribunal stressed that these conditions are not limited to a literal formulation of a given provision, but are rather a result of the axiology of all constitutional provisions.[110]

2.3.5 Essence of social rights and axiology of the Constitution

The concept of the essence of rights, taken from Alexy's theory on constitutional rights, was recognized mostly by the Polish Constitutional Tribunal and the Czech Constitutional Court in their numerous judgments.[111] The Constitutional Tribunal acknowledged that each right and freedom has its core essence (pol.- *rdzeń, jądro*), without which rights neither freedoms could exist. The Tribunal further recognised that both rights and freedoms possess certain additional elements (pol. *otoczka*) that can be formulated and modified without violation of their essence.[112] The very idea of the core essence therefore bears an ambivalent significance implying the negative and/or positive listing of elements[113] that constitute the core every time the given right or freedom is an object of the constitutional review procedure.[114] This is because in general the doctrine accepts

110 P 12/99, *Judgment of 15th November 2000* , p.15-16.

111 In general: W 3/93, *Resolution of 2 March 1994*, OTK part 1, 1994, p.158, W 8/93, *Resolution of 16 march 1994*, OTK part.1 1994, s.165; K 11/95, *Judgment of 26 April 1995*, OTK part 1, 1995, p.132. With reference to social and economic rights, in particular the essence of the right to social security: K 7/90, *Judgment of 2 August 1990*, OTK 1990, p.55; K 14/92, *Judgment of 19 October 1993*, OTK part 2, 1993, p.331; K 8/96, *Judgment of 17 July 1996*, OTK ZU No. 5/1996, p.275; K 7/95, *Judgment of 19 November 1996*, OTK ZU No. 6/1996, p.414; the essence of the right to property in: K 1/91, *Judgment of 28 May 1991*, OTK 1991, p.91.

112 See: P 11/98, *Judgment of 12 January 2000*, concerning "regulated rents" in private buildings, Dz.U. 2000.3.46 of 21 January 2000. Also: SK 9/98, *Judgment of 15 May 1999*, concerning the easement appurtenant, Dz.U. 1999.49.498 of 31 May 1999.

113 See: P 2/98, *Judgment of 12 January 1999*, concerning lawlessness in construction, Dz.U. 1999.3.30 of 15 January 1999.

114 The Tribunal follows this method in cases where it defines the core of the right to social security (ex. K 11/97, K 10/92). In general, the right of the legislator to define the scope of the right to social security concerns, in particular the right to determine an age within

that the essence (core) of a given right or freedom is infringed when provisions of ordinary law obstruct its addresses to the enjoyment of this right or freedom.[115] Though reference to the protection of the core essence is criticized by a claim that it is often an *idem per idem* explanation.[116]

Nevertheless, as mentioned before, the issue of the definition of the core essence is not an exclusive element that gives a meaning to the given right or freedom. It is also the axiology of the Constitution, that is the accompanying provisions that set the grounds for the rights and freedoms inscribed therein. Constitutional social rights, as with all other rights, are supported and surrounded by general constitutional provisions. The understanding of rights is therefore shaped and influenced by other constitutional principles. The place and the way of the formulation of these principles is, in the eyes of constitutional lawyers, as important as enumerated rights in the Constitution.[117] In the doctrine, it is accepted that the importance of constitutional principles[118] when adjudicating in social rights cases is of great importance, since general constitutional principles are a basis and a ratio for an organisation and for the functioning of all of the

a certain period, the limits of which are set by the essence of the right to social security. (See: R. Mizerski, *Kilka uwag o wolnościach i prawach w Konstytucji RP*, in: T. Jasudowicz (ed.), *Polska wobec europejskich standardów praw człowieka*, Toruń 2001, p.23). The method is also used in reference to the right to property (ex. P 11/98), where the Tribunal stated that in order to decide whether the essence of the right to property was protected, an analysis of the sum of the existing limits in the ordinary legislation needs to be performed. In brief, a reference to the basic elements that have shaped the right to property in the course of time influences the understanding of the essence of this right. (See: J. Oniszczuk, *op.cit.*, p.74).

115 B. Banaszak, *Prawa człowieka i obywatela w nowej Konstytucji Rzeczypospolitej Polskiej*, Przegląd Sejmowy No. 5, 1997, p.57.

116 Wojciech Sadurski, *Prawo przed sądem. Studium sądownictwa konstytucyjnego w postkomunistycznych państwach Europy Środkowej i Wschodniej*, Warszawa 2008, p.379.

117 L. Wiśniewski, *Zakres i konstrukcja praw socjalnych w przyszłej konstytucji RP*, in: L. Wiśniewski (ed.), *Podstawowe prawa jednostki i ich ochrona sądowa*, Warszawa 1997, p.90; W. Santera, *Prawa (wolności) pracownicze w Konstytucji*, Praca i Zabezpieczenie Społeczne, No.11, 1997, p.2-7; L. Florek, *Zgodność przepisów prawa pracy z Konstytucją,* Praca i Zabezpieczenie Społeczne, No.11, 1997, p.8-14.

118 Especially with reference to social rights, the principle of the social market economy (art.20), the principle of social justice (together with the principle of proper legislation and materialisation of economic progress, the principle of creation of adequate conditions that allow the beneficiaries of social rights to care for themselves), the principle of sustainable development (art.5), the principles derived from the principle of the rule of law (democratic state ruled by law) and the principles of social justice (art. 2).

constitutional institutions, as well as for the whole system of ordinary laws based in the Constitution.[119]

119 Two constitutional law professors confirmed this point of view during constitutional debates in the Commission of National Assembly. See speeches of: K. Działocha, Komisja Zgromadzenia Narodowego, *Biuletyn VIII*, Warszawa, 1995, p.58, and P. Winczorek, Komisja Zgromadzenia Narodowego, *Biuletyn IX*, Warszawa, 1995, p.54.

PART II

SOCIO-ECONOMIC RIGHTS' CONSTITUTIONALISATION IN POLAND, THE CZECH REPUBLIC AND SLOVAKIA

Chapter 3
Constitutional Debates: Similarities and Differences

The inclusion of social and economic rights in the constitutions of Poland, the Czech Republic and Slovakia was one of the most pertinent issues of the constitutional debates in these countries in the 1990s. The major regime change from communism to democracy mainly intensified discussions over the constitutional enforcement of individual rights in the newborn democracies, what was an expression of a need to guarantee stable and reliable mechanisms that regulate the relationship between the state and individuals. In the early phase of the constitutional debates, largely dominated by emerging political elites,[120] ideologically driven proposals on how to formulate and define constitutional rights were put forward. The scale of socio-economic rights advocacy took different dimensions in these three countries, not only because of the diverging design of constitutional debates but also because of the differences in the structures of the three constitutions. One of the important factors that has influenced the make-up of constitutional debates was perhaps the already mentioned role of political elites in the three countries. Secondly, the timing and the length of debates, which consequently affected the quality of constitutional debates of that time, indirectly influenced the manner in which individual rights have been written in the constitutions. Moreover, organisation of the text of constitutions as well as references and influences of external factors, such as international law, formalized the rights contained therein.

The main characteristics that the three countries' constitutional debates share is not only the general tendency to inscribe individual rights in democratic constitutions, but also to introduce new laws within the framework of social and economic reforms. The latter, was an especially interesting and complex issue as

120 For a detailed study on post-communist elites in Poland, the Czech Republic and Slovakia, their influence and role in the process of constitution drafting see: John Higley, György Lengyel, *Elites after state socialism: theories and analysis*, Rowman & Littlefield, 2000.

it revealed the problem of adjusting laws to the capacities of the in-transition states to provide for certain benefits, but also pointed out the future duties and obligations of the state once it was democraticised. As a consequence, attention has to be paid to the question of the institutional arrangements, and consequences of the introduction of justiciable constitutional social and economic rights. This in turn leads to an interesting study on the way in which constitutional courts have gained their strong position in constitutional interpretation. After all, constitutional courts were the new institutions either introduced by the constitutions, or which started to operate as a result of democratic changes, not having had a strong tradition within the institutional design of the Central and Eastern European states. Were the constitutional provisions so obvious in assigning the courts a privilege of the "last word"? How did the constitutional courts interact with other institutions, contributing thus to overall inter-institutional accountability? And finally, were the Polish, Czech and Slovak Courts active in adjudicating socio-economic cases?

3.1 Socio-Economic Rights Debated

The constitutional discussions took different forms and varied in timings, lengths, actors involved and formulas accepted to organize such debates.[121] In Poland, the debate over the draft constitutional Charter of Rights and Freedoms clearly distinguishing "Social and Economic Rights and Freedoms" from "Economic, Social and Cultural Obligations of Public Authorities" was interrupted by the dissolution of the Parliament that led to new parliamentary elections. In the case of the Czech and Slovak Republics the issue of the division of the country was more important than the actual provisions of fundamental rights, despite the great Czech commitment to the fundamental rights' movement encouraged by Václav Havel. Finally, the Slovak constitutional provisions on fundamental rights are only slightly different from the Czech Charter on Fundamental Rights

121 Poland was the last country among the three under study to have its constitution adopted (1997). The case of the Czech Republic and Slovakia is interesting, since these two countries underwent a separation from one political entity (first Czechoslovakia, and then the Czecho-Slovak Republic). Consequently, the Slovak Constitution was passed in September 1992, while the Czech was adopted in December 1992. Constitutional design was negotiated in Poland between the reformed-communist leadership and the opposition over a period of several months, while the constitutional debates in Czecho-Slovakia were dominated by the political developments and took a form of hasty meetings of the political elites. The focus on social issues and economic reforms in these two countries was therefore put aside until the split of Czecho-Slovakia.

and Basic Freedoms. This not only indicates a poor commitment to the enforcement of human rights at the beginning of the constitutional drafting process, but more importantly has a bearing on the development of the institutional system of promotion and protection of these rights.

The social and economic provisions inscribed in all the three constitutions result from a political compromise conceived under pressing conditions and specific political contexts. Does it imply that social and economic rights lack any axiological or substantive coherence in the constitutions of Poland, the Czech Republic and Slovakia? A short overview of socio-economic constitutional provisions with background indicators to their constitutional fixation should shed a light on the logic according to which this category of rights has been settled down in the three respective constitutions.

3.1.1 Who?- Composition and Role of Political Elites in Constitution Drafting

The social and political change from state socialism encouraged modifications within the political elite, who, during the period of transformation, bore the primary responsibility for framing post-socialist order and played a seminal role in shaping the institutional and legal design of the new democratic regime. It is clearly recognized that the emergence of "new" elites in states governed by democratic constitutions was neither the effect of the replacement of ex-communists by the members of opposition, nor was it the result of the creation of an entirely new political class. Instead, the phenomena of elite circulation, described by Mosca and Pareto,[122] belongs to the various processes accompanying a widely understood democratic transformation. By and large, the political elites in communist Poland and Czechoslovakia oriented themselves towards political, economic and social reforms. The growing importance of opposition and the progressive internal changes in both the Polish and the Czech communist parties that allowed its members to adapt to upcoming democratisation, stimulated the so called "socialism with human face", an orientation towards principles characteristic to democratic regimes, mainly of political liberalisation. Especially after Stalin's era the Party apparatus started to move away from using repression as a primary tool for keeping the power. Likewise, the leadership tried to refer to and reinforce its legitimacy to the population. Notwithstanding the fact that the late communist or rather socialistic regimes to a certain and lim-

122 Gaetano Mosca, The Ruling Class, McGraw-Hill, New York, 1939; Vilfredo Pareto, The Rise and the Fall of Elites, Torowa, New York, 1968.

ited degree turned to legality, it was still unthinkable to assault or to resist the leading role of the Communist Party. Nevertheless, the legal norms the leadership turned to had to become somehow more reliable and realistic. Naturally, changes reached the constitutional level.

In Poland numerous amendments were largely introduced in 1976, and later in 1989 by the so called April Amendment (*nowela kwietniowa*) and the amendments of the contractual parliament,[123] and from 1992 up until 1997 when the new Constitution has been agreed upon, consequently turned the focus from the People's democracy through state socialism to the rule of law. One of the most meaningful amendments concerned the issue of restoration of sovereignty, the abolishment of the formal limitation on sovereignty determined by membership in the Warsaw Pact and dependence on the Soviet Union, as well as the severance of the Brezhnev Doctrine which set the possibilities for internal reforms. These changes authenticated primary constitutional reforms.

Importantly, the first democratic elections in Poland and also in the then-Czechoslovakia did not acknowledge any clear electoral preferences between communists and anti-communists. The results of these elections were rather a proof for a desire to distance the politics from the communist doctrine, but it did not entirely exclude ex-members of the Communist Party from the political scene. Groups of the "reformers" (the reform oriented members of the Communist Part) played a vital role in leading to the negotiated democratic transition, and participated in the subsequent constitutional debates. Being a democrat was not reserved only for the members of the anti-communist opposition, but also became accessible to all who believed in democratisation. In Czechoslovakia it was a number of Prague Spring reformers (the so called: *osmasedesatnik*) together with the 1980s dissidents like Václav Havel that formed the Civic Forum (*Občanske Forum*), a form of a civil society organisation, which then was transformed into a political party and which played a major role in drafting the text of the Czech Constitution, also adopted with some minor changes in Slovakia.[124]

123 Parliament chosen in the first semi-democratic elections where seats were guaranteed to the Communist Party despite of free elections.

124 Note that the Charter of Fundamental Rights and Basic Freedoms was adopted on 16 December 1992 by both the Czech National Council and the Slovak National Council, just a few weeks before the Czech and Slovak Federal Republic ceased to exist. Pursuant to Art.1.2 of the Constitutional Act No. 542/1992 the Czech Republic and Slovakia became the successor states, which implies that the question of legal continuity had to be resolved. By passing a Law on Provisions Connected with the Dissolution of the Czech and Slovak Federal Republic (Constitutional Act of the Czech National Council No. 4/1993 Coll. of 15 December 1992), the Czech Republic assumed all of the obligations arising from interna-

The unity of the Czechoslovak elites was disrupted by the Velvet Divorce in January 1993, with the separation of the major sources of economic conflict between Czech and Slovak Republics. This fact, nevertheless, did not have significant influence on the constitution drafting in Slovakia.

After the June 1990 elections in Czechoslovakia a new Federal Assembly was elected, which then re-elected Václav Havel as President.[125] In September 1990, members of the National Assembly brought into being the Constitutional Commission to draft a new constitution.[126] The competence of the Commission was limited however, since certain sections of the Constitution such as issues dealing with federalism, the bill of rights, and the constitutional courts, were subjected to the competences of the Federal Assembly. It was decided that the Federal Assembly would adopt solutions relevant to the reserved issues by way of amendments to the current Constitution, and that it would incorporate them into the final text of the new constitution.[127]

In Poland, after the first democratic elections in June 1989, the Constitutional Commission of the Polish Parliament (Sejm) was established.[128] According to the principle of proportionality all of the groups present in the Sejm had their representatives in the Commission, although the membership varied and changed because of frequent changes in the compositions of political parties at that time. The Constitutional Commission was composed of three Subcommittees: the Subcommittee on Institutions, charged with designing a new structure of government; the Subcommittee on Social and Economic Provisions, charged with preparing articles dealing with new economic order, issues of property and labour; and the Subcommittee on Human Rights, charged with the preparation of a new bill of rights. The first Committee was dominated by the members of the ex-Communist Party, the PZPR (*Polish United Workers' Party*), while the two others were mainly composed of the Solidarity representatives associated in the

---

tional law in respect of the Czech and Slovak Republic, except for obligations associated with the territory to which the sovereignty of the Czech Republic does not extend, therefore explicitly defining the territorial scope of its legal obligations.

125 Havel became president on December 29, 1989. According to the new election laws, adopted in the spring of 1990, the Federal Assembly re-elected him for the post of the President.

126 The Commission was assisted by a committee of experts.

127 The amendment procedure under the Constitution of 1960 as amended in 1968 predicted that changes required a three-fifths vote of each national delegation in the Chamber of Nations as well as three-fifths of members of the Chamber of the People.

128 The Constitutional Commission was called into being on 7 December 1989.

Civic Parliamentary Club (*Obywatelski Klub Parlamentarny*).[129] The Commission met fifty six times from December 1989 until October 1991, and although it concentrated its works on the issue of the new constitution, it has largely directed its attention to three issues of major importance; namely, on the electoral law for the future parliamentary elections, constitutional amendments (what inhibited the Commission members from working on merits), and on the question of a constitutional referendum. The main issues discussed in the Subcommittee on Social and Economic Provisions concerned the principle of social justice[130] and the question of the actual inscription of socio-economic rights within the new constitution. While the first issue helped to find a common ground for fur-

129 According to Wiktor Osiatyński, one of the Constitutional Commission's external experts, insomuch as most important constitutional reforms concerning the change of the political system have already been approved in the Small Constitution, the majority of seats in the Sub-Committee on the Institutions were offered to the ex-communists in order to allow the parliamentarians who had descended from the opposition to sit in the two other Subcommittees. Consequently, Osiatyński claims that by assigning chairmanship to the Solidarity descendants, members of the OKP- Andrzej Zawiślak (and then to Anna Dynowska) in the Subcommittee on Social and Economic Provisions, and Hanna Suchocka in the Subcommittee on Human Rights- it had been assured that the creation of a new socio-economic system would first envisage protection of reforms commenced by the then Minister of Finance Leszek Balcerowicz, and second that in this way it renders the domain of human rights protection and promotion to the representatives of the Solidarity movement, which considered fundamental human rights as a basic principle in its fight against the communist regime. See in: Ryszard Chruściak, Wiktor Osiatyński, *Tworzenie Konstytucji w Polsce w latach 1989-1997*, Instytut Spraw Publicznych, 2001,p. 14-15. Andrzej Rapaczyński, another external expert of the Subcommittee on Institutions, also records the fact that most of the members of this Committee were tied to the old regime. He admits that except for a few expatriate experts associated with the new regime others were recruited from the once-tightly controlled university's law faculties. Despite of Solidarity concerns over the work of this crucial Committee, in Rapaczyński's opinion, the Committee managed to distance itself from the communist loyalties and worked quite harmoniously to draft the best possible proposals for the sections of the Constitution dealing with the composition and functioning of the parliament, the government, the presidency, and the judiciary. See in: Andrzej Rapaczyński, *Constitutional Politics in Poland: A Report on the Constitutional Committee of the Polish Parliament*, University of Chicago Law Review, No.58, 1991, p.603

130 The principle of social justice as one of the constitutional principles, which should be taken into account in the new Constitution was discussed on the plenum of the Commission for the first time in February 1990. See: Komisja Konstytucyjna Zgromadzenia Narodowego. Builetyn I, Wydawnictwo Sejmowe, Warszawa 1991

ther discussion,[131] the latter resulted in a clear division of opinions and convictions. Notwithstanding the general tendency of democratisation supported by political elites- both ex-communist and opposition- questions on the legitimacy of representatives who drafted the democratic Constitution of Poland and Czechoslovakia (then of the Czech Republic and of the Slovak Republic) arose not only in public debates but also amongst the elites. The question of struggle for power prevailed over constitutional merits, and what consequently provoked either lengthy doctrinal disputes in Poland,[132] in Czechoslovakia resulted in the rapid initiative of a group of politicians to draft the Constitution overnight.

In Poland especially, there was considerable controversy over the fact that the Contractual Sejm was not a product of fully free elections.[133] With the preponderance of the ex-communist deputies, the Sejm was not considered to be fully legitimate to give expression of the will of the Polish people. When recalling in 1995 the works of the Constitutional Commission its President Bronisław Geremek said in one of the interviews that the first Parliament was least democratic from among the Parliaments he has worked in but had a sense of original sin and therefore functioned differently. Nevertheless, in his view, it worked most efficiently for the democracy.[134] Rapaczyński, one of the Commission's experts, on the other hand

131 Ryszard Chruściak, Wiktor Osiatyński, *op.cit.,* p.19-23. During constitutional debates in the Commission both the principle of social justice and the role of work in societal life were most commonly referred to as a manifestation of the rapprochement between socialist doctrine and the Catholic Church's social teaching. Paradoxically, even though traditionally communists showed reluctance and aversion to the Catholic social teaching, it was easier for the post-communist socialists to find a common language in this sphere with catholic groupings rather than with the followers of liberalism.

132 Mostly however, attention from the merits on constitutional rights shifted to the power-relations dispute when Lech Wałęsa became the first president of the Republic of Poland and when he and the Solidarity forces around him lobbied for a strong presidency system. The Solidarity movement was divided in this respect, since the so called Warsaw group favoured the Chancellor system. In this sense, issues under jurisprudence of the Constitutional Committee were often politicised and watered down the Commission's importance.

133 Contrary then to the Sejm, the June elections to the Senat (the upper Chamber of the Parliament) were entirely free. As a result Senat was predominantly composed of the Solidarity representatives. This as a matter of fact became yet another factor which gave a reason to weaken Sejm's Constitutional Commission. Namely, the Senate, with a sense of its greater legitimacy, formed its own Constitutional Commission and began to work on a separate draft of the Constitution.

134 See: Witkor Osiatyński, *An Argument against Popular Ratification and for Chancellor Democracy. Bronislaw Geremek on constitution-making in Poland. Interview with Bronisław Geremek*, EECR, Vol.4, Nr.1 1995, pp.42-45, p.45.

claims that the Sejm was perhaps more representative than if the elections had been entirely free and the Solidarity dominated Senate was a good example of it. Moreover, the unelected but contracted members of the Sejm not only introduced some variety to its composition, but they also tried to prove that the dubious legitimacy of their position made them exercise great care in opposing the Solidarity-dominated parliamentary leadership.[135] Consequently, a doubt on the legitimacy of the drafters resulted in questioning the legality of the resultant text of the Constitution. In order to overcome this obscurity it was decided (mainly by the Solidarity leadership in the Parliament) that after the draft of the Constitution was being completed by the Constitutional Commission, the National Assembly would approve the new constitution by a two-thirds majority and then submit it to a national referendum. Although technically the referendum was non-binding, it gave the new constitution the legitimacy derived from direct popular approval. Ratification of the Constitution through a broad participation of the political elite and the society was thought to confer legitimacy on the text.[136]

3.1.2 When and How?- Time and Length of Constitutional Debates

During the early stages of the constitutional debate in Poland, Sejm's Constitutional Commission met in plenary sessions and discussed the general principles of the new constitutional order, the relationship between Polish domestic law and international law, and the basic types of individual rights that were to be included in the new Constitution. Subcommittees met to discuss more detailed issues within their competences and subsequently sent the results to the Commission. The upper Chamber of the Parliament, the Senat has also initiated works on the new Constitution. Nevertheless, little attention has been given to its work, because no party leaders (including Solidarity's) approved its formation. Consequently, the Sejm's Commission managed to retain its position and continued to work on the constitutional project. Yet, the Senat's initiative was also questioned as to its legitimacy, since the 1952 Constitution placed the matter of constitutional changes to the Sejm. The role of the Senat was clarified in a statute

---

135 Andrzej Rapaczyński, *Constitutional Politics in Poland...*, p.603-604.

136 Still, predominant political tensions and the focus on consensus building was not perhaps the best solution for the drafting of the Constitution. See again the interview with Bronisław Geremek in: An Argument against Popular Ratification ...EECR Vol. 4 Nr 1 1995 pp.42-45, p.43. Geremek assesses from a time perspective that "compromise should not shape the actual drafting of the constitution but [...] it should be an aspect of the general political conditions, preceding the constitution-making process". Subsequently he ascertains that in such circumstances, constitution should be passed when conflicts are at minimum and the chances for agreement are greatest.

passed in the fall of 1990, specifying that the two Chambers of Parliament sitting together as a National Assembly would approve the constitution. Eventually, the Senat did not debate its final proposal presented on 24 October 1991 because of growing tensions between parties under the Solidarity movement. Instead, it adopted a resolution stating that the project would be handed over to the Parliament in the next term.[137] After the end of the first cadence of the Parliament non of the Commissions' projects, neither Sejms' nor Senat's, were put to the vote in their respective chambers. The Parliament's failure to enact new, democratic Constitution resulted from several reasons comprehensively recorded by Chruściak and Osiatyński in their account of the Polish constitutional debate. The first reason recognised the fiasco as an inherent to the character of transformation and to a certain extent inevitable. Second puts the blame on the politicians and drafters of the attempted constitution, especially in that they provoked the creation of the two Commissions and consequently of the two different projects. All that cleary hampered the decision-making process.[138]

The Charter of Fundamental Rights and Basic Freedoms was adopted in Czechoslovakia on January 9, 1991 by the required super-majority of the Federal Assembly members. The Charter was a result of a "long process of legislative deliberation, controversy and compromise that reflected the differing cultural, socio-political, and ideological persuasions and aspirations of the deputies to Czechoslovakia's three parliaments. The Charter was preceded by several working drafts, one of which passed both the Czech and Slovak National Councils. The National Councils then presented a harmonized version to the Federal Assembly, which adopted it with a few more modifications."[139]

---

137 See; Prace Komisji Konstytucyjnej Senatu, Zeszyt 5, p. 182

138 Ryszard Chruściak, Wiktor Osiatyński, *Tworzenie Konstytucji w Polsce...*, p.62-76. Rightly, the authors point to the fact that many parliamentarians were members of other constitutional commissions, which have contributed to the politisation of the works of constitutional Commissions in the Parliament. Namely, mixing the role of the politician and the constitution drafter often led to the subordination of the future Constitution to current political interests. As the most prominent example they bring up the case of the conflict over regulations concerning electoral law. Works on the constitution waived for over three months. Escalation of the conflict between Sejm and President Wałęsa efficiently dominated the works of the Sejms' Constitutional Commission and definitely squander the chances for constitution-making over political interests.

139 Lloyd Cutler, Herman Schwartz, *Constitutional Reform in Czechoslovakia: E Duobus Unum?*, University of Chicago Law Review, No. 58, 1991, p.531

3.1.3 Where and Where From?- Structure and Reference to the Constitutional Text

The Czech Charter is often described as a prompt response by the Czechoslovak Parliament to the expectations and demands of the public to immediately protect basic human rights and freedoms guaranteed by the previous regime.[140] Inspiration to the Charter was drawn from the ideals of the interwar republic and the 1920 Constitution, mostly with reference to the legislative and institutional forms. The Bill also incorporates principles of the European Charter of Human Rights. Indeed, the reference to the Convention was made in view of the prompt accession of Czechoslovakia to the Council of Europe. Clear commitments to European human rights' values were envisaged by the Czechoslovak authorities as proof of the country's "return to Europe".[141] In this context Přiban points out the legitimisation issue as an important premise that influenced political and legal reconstruction in Czechoslovakia and later in the Czech Republic. The dissident "legalistic" strategy manifested in the reliance on international human rights treaties which served to demonstrate the immoral nature of the communist regime.[142] Controversy around economic and social rights did not provoke that many discussions as in Poland. Inclusion of these rights seemed to be obvious for the Czechoslovak elites, not only owing to ECHR references, but largely with regard to ensuring the credibility of the Charter itself. Social and economic rights were already guaranteed in the 1920 Constitution, and back then they were considered as an important factor in modern democracy.[143] Moreover, the elites involved in the process of Charter drafting were concerned about sustaining its viability and made sure that the social guarantees of the previous regime were also addressed in the new bill of rights.

---

140 Lloyd Cutler, Herman Schwartz, *ibid.*, p.531

141 See: Speech of Jri Dienstbier, Czechoslovak Foreign Minister addressing the Council of Europe, Membership Approved, Foreign Broadcast Information Service –East Europe, Daily Report East Europe 12, January 13, 1991, cited after: Lloyd Cutler, Herman Schwartz, *ibid.*, fn50 at p.532.

142 Jiří Příbáň, James Young, *The Rule of Law in Central Europe. The Reconstruction of Legality, Constitutionalism and Civil Society in the Post-Communist Countries,* Aldeshot, Brookfield, Singapore, Sydney, Ashgate 1999, p.29-55.

143 In the comments to the 1920 Constitution Edward Taborsky (a secretary to the second President of the First Republic, Edward Benes) argues that "economic and social rights are an increasingly important factor in modern democracy. Any Constitution that overlooks them, as do almost all existing Constitutions, is bound to be defective. E. Taborsky, *Czechoslovak Democracy at Work*, George Allen & Unwin, 1945, p.130-131, cited after: Lloyd Cutler, Herman Schwartz, *ibid.*, fn 63 at p.535

The early works of the Constitutional Commission in Poland and of its Subcommittee on Social and Economic Provisions, gives the most coherent picture of the discussion on constitutionalisation of social rights within the new democratic order. While the Constitutional Commission evenly discussed the proposals drafted in the Subcommittees, most of the uncertainties and conflicts came from the dispute within the Human Rights Subcommittee and the Socio and Economic Provisions Subcommittee over social and economic constitutional issues. The two committees assumed different philosophical grounds which affected the proposals to the Commission on the issue. The Subcommittee on Human Rights under the chairmanship of Hanna Suchocka, sought a compromise between social-democratic heritage and principles of the social teaching of the Catholic Church.[144] On the other hand, the Subcommittee on Social and Economic Provisions led by Andrzej Zawiślak based its proposals on liberal grounds.[145] Fundamental disagreement concerned the question to what extent, if ever, should social and economic provisions be inscribed in the constitution. On the one hand it was claimed that the constitution should contain a universal catalogue of rights and freedoms which would not pre-define the socio-economic regime of the state. It was understood that civil and political rights would constitute the basic catalogue of constitutional human rights from within which individuals would have their social and economic rights protected. In addition, the

144 The social teaching of the Catholic Church (most commonly referred as Catholic social teaching) addresses aspects of Catholic doctrine relating to collective welfare of humanity. Its foundations have been laid by Pope Leo XIII's 1981 encyclical letter *Rerum Novarum*, although it was Pope Pius XI in the encyclical letter *Quadragesimo Anno* of 1931 who has further developed the foundations of this thought. Catholic social teaching largely refers to matters such as: life and human dignity; family, community and participation; rights and duties; respect for elderly and poor; dignity in work and labour rights; solidarity. From within constitutional commissions in the Polish Parliament, the Senat's Commission (mainly because the engagement of its President, Alicja Grześkowiak) was to a large extent engaged in the dialogue with the representatives of the Catholic Church. Ultimately, Senat's constitutional project referred to the principle of solidarism (as outlined in the Catholic social teaching), which, as opposed to the liberal conception of law, constitutes a basis for guarantees of rights and freedoms not only to individuals but also to communities (*solidaryzm społeczny*). Likewise, recognition of the "common good" (*dobro wspólne)* was included in the Senat's Commission project. The common good was recognized as a guiding principle for the execution of constitutionally guaranteed rights and freedom, and its reference envisaged a criterion for permissible limitations by a statute of rights to private property and the freedom to undertake economic activity. See discussions of the Senat's Commission on the common good and principle of solidarism in: *Prace Komisji Konstytucyjnej Senatu*, Zeszyt 5, p.55, 169.

145 Komisja Konstytucyjna Zgromadzenia Narodowego, *Biuletyn IX*, Wydawnictwo Sejmowe, Warszawa 1991, s.14-15

principles of the socio-economic regime would be derived from concrete constitutional provisions on individual rights.[146] On the other hand, others postulated the inclusion of social and economic provisions which could enrich the axiological sphere of the basic text. The second controversy concerned social rights. Should they be enclosed in the Constitution at all? And if yes, where exactly in the text should they find their place? Opinions varied from the positive claims in constitutionalising social rights and placing them in separate chapters, to warnings and concerns that these rights once enshrined in the constitution would cause difficulties for the courts when implementing the constitution.[147]

The argument of the communist heritage is often raised in discussions on the source of socio-economic rights in democratic Constitutions.[148] It is true to a

146 Controversy over the inclusion of socio-economic provisions as basic constitutional principles was also discussed in the Senat's Constitutional Commission, which finally decided that it should not be the case. One of the expert reports presented by Jerzy Stępień argued that the future socio-economic regime is hard to predict, therefore inclusion of such provisions in the Constitution would only lead to direct definition of the socio-economic order by the drafters of the Constitution, what should be avoided. Moreover, Stępień reaffirmed the Sejm's Constitutional Commission's conviction that it is very difficult to distinguish the concepts of constitutional principles that describe the socio-economic order and the actual rights and duties of citizens. See: *Prace Komisji Konstytucyjnej Senatu*, Zeszyt 4, p. 129.

147 The Senat's proposal contained some social and economic rights and freedoms. Nevertheless, it did not provide for a developed catalogue of these rights, mainly by raising the argument that the execution of these rights is ineffective and impossible, what was proven by the previous constitutional regime. Moreover, it has been feared that enforcement of socio-economic rights downgrade effective execution of all constitutional rights. Ipso facto, inclusion of socio-economic rights in the Constitution would disturb direct applicability of constitutional provisions. See: *Prace Komisji Konstytucyjnej Senatu*, Zeszyt 4, p. 60, 174. Another aspect of efficient enforceability of constitutional rights was raised with respect to the introduction of the enforcement mechanisms. Senate's project proposed that judicial protection of constitutional rights is guaranteed to everyone whose rights and freedoms recognised by the Constitution were violated. The violation could also result from the action of individuals who have acted in a public capacity. The project however, did not envisage other means of rights protection, nor did it provide for the right to compensation in cases of violation. It did not envisage constitutional individual complaint to the Constitutional Tribunal, but it did foresee the right to petition the Ombudsman in case of violation of individual rights by state organs.

148 Among others: Wojciech Sadurski, *Rights Before Courts. A Study of Constitutional Courts in Post-communist States of Central and Eastern Europe*, Springer, 2005; J.-M. Henckearts, S. Van Der Jeught, *Human Rights Protection Under the New Constitutions of Central Europe*, Loyola of Los Angeles International & Comparative Law Journal, 1998.

certain extent that the communist and then socialistic doctrine took profound roots in the Central Eastern European consciousness. The legally regulated equalisation of societal positions in past regimes,[149] although founded on lofty ideas of communism/socialism suddenly crashed with significant visible divisions and inequalities in the society undergoing socio-economic transformation. Disregard to constitutionally guaranteed social and economic rights and freedoms would only discredit political elites in such circumstances. It was not evident however, that these rights should remain within the new democratic Constitutions. As previously illustrated, the debates on socio-economic rights constitutionalisation, especially in Poland, brought about two opposite opinions.

In contrast, there was also another significant argument, which is often forgotten or omitted in the literature. It is namely the constitutional reality and the activity of the Constitutional Courts that have contributed to the final victory of social and economic rights depicted as constitutional rights in most of the Central Eastern European Constitutions. While observing the constitutional debates, however, one has an impression that although the social pressure was significant and had a direct implication on the acknowledgement of the legitimacy of new political elites to enact new Constitutions, the dominant group that was actually preoccupied by the issue of constitutionalisation of socio-economic rights, was the political elite. Moreover, as it was shown above, the issue although recognised as important, was either easily abandoned when institutional disputes arose (like in Poland), or were simply conferred to one political group (like in Czechoslovakia).

3.1.4 What did we come with? – Results of Constitutional Debates

In the Polish Constitution of 1997, freedoms, rights and obligations of persons and citizens are derived from general principles defined in Articles 30-37. General principles enable the definition not only of the scope of application of freedoms, rights and obligations but, more importantly, indicate the three fundamental sources which constitute a basis for the entire set of rights and freedoms.[150]

149 The equalisation stemmed from the doctrinal assumption that members of socialistic (communist) society are equal in all domains of social, political, economic life. Justification of this thesis was derived from the guiding principle of the socialistic (communist) doctrine, claiming that the equalisation is implemented in the name of building socialism, and it predetermined socialistic affiliation of all citizens of a socialistic state.

150 Lech Garlicki, *Constitutional Law*, in: S. Frankowski (ed.), *Introduction to Polish Law*, 2005, p.11-17.

First is the principle of the dignity of a person (Art.30).[151] Although placed at a supra-constitutional universal ground, it has not been elaborated by the judiciary more frequently than the principle of a democratic state ruled by law (Art.2). Yet, in the Polish constitutional doctrine the principle of the dignity of a person gives an inborn and irrevocable source of freedom and guarantees rights to individuals. Second, the principle of freedom (arts.31.1, 31.2) which ensures the respect of freedoms and rights of others, as well as of the idea that no one should be compelled to do something that is not required by law. Third, the principle of equality (Art.32) which is relatively frequently referred to in the Polish constitutional jurisprudence. It expresses equality before the law, the right to equal treatment by public authorities, prohibition of discrimination in political, social, and economic life or for any reason whatsoever. Moreover, subsequent articles of the general principles section provide for the equality of men and women (Art.33), equal legal protection regarding ownership, other property rights and the right of succession (Art.64.2), as well as equality in the context of elections (Art. 96.2, Art. 169.2). In addition, a separate provision grants equal rights of churches and other religious organisations (Art.25.1). As to social and economic rights themselves they are stipulated in Subtitle IV of the Constitution, and are derived from the three above mentioned fundamental principles. According to Art.67.1, for example, while asserting the right to social security, particular attention should be addressed to ill, old or disabled people. This being an example of an extension of the principle of equal opportunities, since the guarantee of equal rights is an essential precondition of the principle in question. Anti-discrimination laws should be adapted in this respect, and they should relate to vulnerable groups of people who are exposed to discrimination.

Although a separate constitutional act which comprises fundamental rights and freedoms has been adopted in the Czech Republic, pursuant to Art. 3 of the Constitution it constitutes an integral component of the constitutional order of the Czech Republic. In this respect the Czech solution differs from the Polish and Slovak, in a way that it separates the fundamental rights from the main text of the constitution. It does not have, however, any negative legal impact on the validity or positioning of these rights within the constitutional order. On the contrary, the Charter enjoys the binding force of constitutional law and is at the top of the pyramid of the legal order. The Charter of Fundamental Rights and Basic Freedoms (CFRBF) gives a detailed insight into human rights protection, explicitly specifying social and cultural rights in Chapter 4. The form of the CFRBF

151 The principle of dignity is also mentioned in the Preamble of the Polish Constitution of 1997.

reflects the intentions of the Federal Assembly to legislate not only a political proclamation, but also a positive legal regulation in a comprehensive sense.[152] In this respect, human rights and fundamental freedoms, as provided for in the main text of the Constitution (Art.87.1d of the Constitution), are under the protection of the Constitutional Court. Such protection is not exclusive, since any ordinary court provides for the protection for human rights (Art.36 of the Charter). Also, attention has been paid to formulate the rights and freedoms in such a way as to guarantee real, substantive, and enforceable rights. The differences in enforceability between fundamental rights and freedoms and the economic and social rights have been recognised and subjected to reservations provided for in Article 41 of the Charter, which states that some of the Charter's social and economic rights are only enforceable to the extent provided for by legislation that implements these rights.

Fundamental rights and freedoms in the Constitution of the Slovak Republic are derived from the same Federal Charter of Fundamental Rights and Basic Freedoms. In contrast to the Czech solution, the provisions of fundamental rights protection in the Slovak Constitution were incorporated in the Constitution itself, namely in Part Two entitled "Fundamental Rights and Freedoms". It follows and at several points expands the already invalid Federal Charter provisions.[153] The Charter, however, remains still in force as a separate, federal (sic!) constitutional act. Such a twofold reflection of the human rights provisions in the Slovak constitutional order remains an exceptionally interesting case of the legal arrangement.

---

152 See: D. Jíek, M. Hoffmann, *Czech Republic*, in: R. Blackburn, J. Polakiewicz (eds.), *Fundamental Rights in Europe. The European Convention on Human Rights and its Member States*, 2001, p.242; Lloyd Cutler, Herman Schwartz, *op.cit.*, p.536.

153 Entitlements of employment, for example within the Federal Charter were captured in a simple contestation that the working conditions should be "satisfactory" with details to be further set by a separate law. In the Slovak Constitution this idea is developed by enumerating seven categories of entitlements, including, for instance the setting of a maximum number of working hours, a reasonable rest time after work and a minimum amount of paid vacation. Such extensive wording is seen as a broadening of the general provision which consequently leads to a blurring of its meaning. A positive interpretation of the constitutional provision in the same constitutional act itself, which includes a detailed scope of its interpretation, apart from being fuzzy, is widely contested. The strengthening of economic and social rights in this case is seen as making these rights practical as opposed to theoretical. For more details see: E. Stein, *Czecho/Slovakia. Ethnic Conflict, Constitutional Fissure, Negotiated Breakup*, University of Michigan Press, 1997, p.279-280.

3.2 Placing Limits on Socio-Economic Constitutional Rights

The Czech and Slovak constitutional acts contain a general clause which envisages a separation of socio-economic rights from other rights by submitting most of these rights to the limits of laws enacted to implement them. In the case of Poland, the distinction over enforceability of rights is carried out within socio-economic rights themselves, meaning that on the one hand, there are some rights which are directly enforceable (even though some of them are subject to a clause which explicitly delegates the duty to determine the scope and form of their implementation to the legislature, ex. the right to social security).[154] Yet on the other hand, there are some which are conditioned by legislative discretion.[155]

When comparing social and economic constitutional provisions provided for in the constitutional orders of Poland, the Czech Republic and Slovakia on the basis of their direct enforceability, two categories of constitutional provisions can be identified:

a) rights, whose enforceability is conditioned by legislative discretion in all three constitutional acts (these include labour relation rights, such as the right to minimum wage, full employment, hygienic conditions of work and the right to days free from work; rights to housing and protection of the family);
b) rights which are directly enforceable by the constitution in Poland but are conditioned or not mentioned[156] by Czech and Slovak constitutional acts (this category encompasses property rights, right to social security, right to health care, right to free education, rights of the child, and freedom of artistic creation and scientific research, aid to the disabled, protection of consumers and customers).

The three constitutions recognize in this way that most social and economic rights require policy choices by the legislative and the executive. The previous

154 Art. 67 of the Polish Constitution.

155 For the general clause see: Art. 81 Polish Constitution. This case relates to the rights to a minimum wage (Art.65.4), full employment (Art.65.5), hygienic conditions of work and the right to days free from work (Art.66), aid to disabled persons provided for the public authorities (Art.69), protection of the family (Art.71), ecological security and protection of the environment (Art.74), the right to housing (Art.75), and finally the protection of consumers and customers (Art.76).

156 E.g. right to housing is not guaranteed in the Czech Charter of Fundamental Rights and Basic Freedoms.

information requires that all among social and economic rights in the Czech and in Slovak constitutions, and some in the Polish constitution are subject to the discretion of a legislator. But is the constitutional challenge to socio-economic laws and policies therefore limited? It is clear that the same recognition of positive rights does not entitle individuals to claim some of them from the state. By referring to a set of social and economic rights as the limiting clause, states have secured themselves a place in public social and economic policies which are under their own discretion, since these rights may only be claimed within the scope of laws implementing them. It does not however, undermine the normative character of rights in question, and leaves a well-grounded and justified field for constitutional review.

Since constitutional socio-economic rights bring about the issue of far-reaching judicial interference in the politics and competences of the legislators, there is at least an intuitive endeavour to limit the consequences of the effects constitutional socio-economic rights bring.[157] This intuition is supported by the belief in specific nature of constitutional socio-economic rights, namely in their vertical reference. The vertical reference stands for the protection of the fiscal interests of the State. Combined together, the intuition and budgetary reality, bring about a tension and in fact inevitably lead to the necessary declaration as to what axiological preferences constitutional drafters are in favour of. These tensions could have been observed during constitutional debates in Poland and Czechoslovakia. In view of this, the so called limitation clauses were added to the Constitutions and in the case of Polish, Czech and Slovak Constitutions specifically refer to socio-economic rights. There are differences, however, between the accepted solutions that consequently exert the effect on the nature of socio-economic rights.

It is often claimed that the nature of socio-economic rights require legal-constitutional limitations in order to allow their materialisation. Certainly, they are mostly claim rights, the materialisation of which would require significant financial contribution from the state budget. Moreover, the problem of the distribution of benefits, in case these rights are considered fully justiciable, brings about problems of equality and social justice. Therefore, it is claimed that the limitations on constitutional socio-economic rights stem from their nature- imprecise and with the scope of these rights dependent on the one hand on the available resources needed for their materialisation, and on the other resultant

157 T. Gizbert-Studnicki, A. Grabowski, *Normy programowe w Konstytucji*, in: J. Trzciński (ed.) Charakter i struktura norm Konstytucji, 1997.

from relatively new constitutional interpretation and use of these rights.[158] As previously mentioned, the way in which these limitations are formulated result in diverging legal consequences. In general the distinction concerns *general limitation clauses* provided for by a separate article which results in indirect applicability of a given right or freedom. And in opposition, *concrete limitation clauses* inscribed in a concrete article which relates to direct reference to statutory law as a source of the content and extent of a given right/freedom. The latter clause delegates the duty to determine the scope and form of implementation to the legislature. The three Constitutions- Polish, Czech and Slovak, contain both general and concrete limitation clauses. Formulation of general limitation clauses, however, influences the significance of concrete limitation clauses which is different between then Polish and Czech and Slovak case.

In the **Polish Constitution** the general limitation clause is provided for by Article 81. This clause enumerates specific but not all socio-economic rights guaranteed in the Constitution which may be asserted only in the limits specified by statute. Accordingly, it refers to a minimum level of remuneration (Art.65(4)), public policies which aim to provide full employment (Art.65(5)), right to safety at work and statutory specified days free from work (Art.66), provision on aid to disabled persons (Art.69), protection of the family and special assistance to pregnant women (Art.71), provision concerning ecological security and protection of environment (Art.74), satisfaction of housing needs and protection of rights of tenants (Art.75), and finally, provision guaranteeing protection of consumers and customers (Art.76). This means that legislative restrictions imposed on these specific rights depend on the will of the legislator and the constitutional formulation of a given right cannot be regarded as a direct basis for individual claim.[159] The legal meaning of these rights is therefore weakened, as the scope of claims is limited. Moreover, it stems clearly from the formulation of these rights, and it is confirmed by the general limitation clause, that the addressee of the constitutional provision subject to Art. 81 is the state. Therefore, individual enforcement of these rights is impossible. The limitation is being imposed on the direct applicability of these rights in a way that the possibility of formulation of claims of unconstitutionality of acts and policies that

158 See: Przemysław Mikłaszewicz, *op.cit.,* p.108 According to the author, the uncertainty as to what are the consequences of full justiciability of constitutional socio-economic rights is a direct reason why these rights are subject to limitation clauses on the constitutional level, which were not concreted at the ordinary legislature level.

159 See for example Decision of the Polish Constitutional Tribunal K 11/00 with reference to Article 71 which stipulates a general obligation of the state to take into account the good of the family in its social and economic policy.

materialize these provisions is restricted. From this it follows that such constitutional guarantees become programmatic norms.[160] It does not mean, however, that rights which are bound by the general limitation clause cannot be referred to as a basis for a constitutional review. It is unclear, however, whether all types of constitutional review can be implemented in this respect. Some claim that these rights, while not the grounds for individual complaint, can be subject to constitutional abstract review.[161] Others, include constitutional individual complaint as a possible type of constitutional review in this case, although, as already mentioned, individual claims are restricted.[162] So far, it is confirmed both by the doctrine and by the case law that the legislator cannot arbitrarily limit rights and freedoms guaranteed by the Constitution, nor it can depart from the essence[163] that forms the nature of these rights. In this case the doctrine extended enforceability of constitutional socio-economic rights which are subject to limitation clause stemming from Article 81. Yet, the Constitution can not be the sole basis of the claim. The statutory provision needs to be adduced.[164]

How is it different therefore from the effects that specific limitation clauses have on these socio-economic rights which are not subject to the general clause? A general difference stems from the fact that the content of a right that is not

160 See: Decision of the Polish Constitutional Tribunal SK 22/99.

161 Wojciech Sadurski, *Constitutional Socio-Economic Rights: Lessons from Central Europe*, in: Workshop of the Foundation for Law, Justice and Society, Oxford 2008 (unpublished). Copy with the autor.

162 Leszek Garlicki, *Polskie prawo konstytucyjne. Zarys wykładu*, Liber,2006, p.116

163 The essence of rights and freedoms originates in Polish constitutionalism from the German constitutional tradition (*Wesensgehalt*). It is assumed that each of the constitutional rights and freedoms has its own essence (core), which defines given right/freedom. Apart from the essence they also have certain elements that may be changed and modified without infringing the core of the right/freedom (entourage). The idea of the core of rights and/or freedoms stems from Art.31(3), sentence 2, which stipulates that any limitations to the constitutional rights and freedoms shall not violate their essence. The most prominent example of the Polish constitutional case law with respect to the essence of constitutional socio-economic rights is the case concerning failed valorisation of rents and old-age pensions for certain period which infringed the core of the right to social security, Decision of the Polish Constitutional court from 17 July 1996, K 8/96 (which will be referred to in detail in the next Chapter).

164 See: Leszek Garlicki, *ibid.*; also Decision of the Polish Constitutional Tribunal P 3/05, in which the Tribunal said that Article 71.1 sentence 2 (which provides for a right to special assistance from public authorities to families in difficult material and social circumstances) expresses a subjective right which is subject to individual constitutional complaint.

subject to the general limitation clause is directly shaped by the constitutional norm. These rights may still be limited by a concrete clause which conditions them to provisions provided for by ordinary law (statutes). This indeed means that the obligations of the legislator resulting from this constitutional provision are stronger than those which are subject to the general limitation clause. The general conclusion is that Art.81 of the Polish Constitution specifies socio-economic rights which are characterised by programmatic norms, while the rest of these rights can be directly enforced on the basis of the Constitution.

In digression it needs to be noted that constitutional social rights in Poland are a result of a compromise reached during the constitutional debates in the 1990s. This compromise is reflected in the way that social rights are formulated, as well as in their placement in the chapters and titles of the constitution.

Article 41 in the **Czech Charter** provides for a general limitation clause which encompasses almost all socio-economic rights. The provision provides an exception to the general rule that the Charter is directly applicable and to the situation when rights are claimed on this basis should be in direct reference to the Charter. This limitation applies to the rights enumerated in Art.41, which apart from being covered by the general limitation clause contain further restrictions. This means, that the rights subject to the general provision may be enforced only within the limits defined by the law which develops given rights. It is acknowledged by the doctrine that these rights have the character of natural rights as stipulated in Article 1 of the Charter[165] and in the Universal Declaration of Human Rights. Therefore their materialisation is subject to both Article 1 and Article 36 (1), but their enforceability is limited to the confines established by ordinary legislation.[166] That is to say that ordinary laws cannot go beyond the extent to which the rights are laid out in the Charter, nor can they deny them. An example of the latter situation, i.e. a case when the Constitutional Court found that the right to free education, stipulated in Article 33(2), was denied, is to be found in the so called *School Tuition case* **Pl. ÚS 35/93.**[167] In its decision the Court annulled the parliamentary amendment of Act No. 29/1984 Sb. on the System of the Primary and Secondary Schools. The Court found that the Act threatened the development of the constitutionally guaranteed free elementary

165 Article 1 of the Czech Charter says: All people are free, have equal dignity, and enjoy equality of rights. Their fundamental rights and basic freedoms are inherent, inalienable, non-prescriptible, and not subject to repeal. (original translation) http://angl.concourt.cz/angl_verze/rights.php

166 V. Pavlíček (ed.), *Ústava a ústavní řád České republiky. Komentář. 2. díl Práva a svobody*, Line, Praha 2002, p.338

167 Pl. ÚS 35/93, Published under 49.1994 Sb.

and secondary school education by subjecting it to the general rule that education on these levels is free "unless otherwise provided for by statute".[168] The Court found the quoted clause in clear opposition to the essence and purpose of the constitutional right to education, and considered it unconstitutional. In this case the Court observed that despite the acceptable limits on the right to education, its nature and meaning must be preserved. Therefore, although the interpretation of a given right was narrowed down, it still needs to be effectively materialised accordingly to Art.41 which stipulates that the laws which materialise specific rights need to guarantee their effective performance (*ustanovení musí být zákony skutečně provedena*).

In conclusion, according to the Polish doctrine, both claim rights and programmatic norms have the full normative power of constitutional provisions. In this sense, the Polish hybrid solution assumes that where some social rights may be asserted subject to limitations specified by law, others are directly enforceable even if they have their own limitation clauses that refer to the duty to determine the scope and form of implementation to the legislature. The Czech approach favours a vision of social rights that assumes they are objective rather than subjective rights. Slovak doctrine, on the other hand accepted a more universal approach in this regard.

3.3 Constitutional Mechanisms of Enforcement of Socio-Economic Rights

3.3.1 Leading/Prevailing Role of Constitutional Courts

As mentioned above, the early activity of the Constitutional Courts has contributed, to a certain extent, to the constitutionalisation of socio-economic rights. The communist/socialistic legacy, was not only reflected in popular expectations that these rights were inscribed in the Constitution, but was also as a result of the direct influence of the constitutional heritage. In Poland the activity of the Constitutional Tribunal took place before the final text of the democratic Constitution was enacted. The Tribunal therefore in its numerous judgements either interpreted the rights stipulated in the 1952 Constitution with a reference to the *democratic constitutional reality*, or derived certain rights from the new constitutional principles that have already created the new democratic constitutional

168 Pl. ÚS 35/93, Published under 49.1994 Sb. and CESCR, 'Replies by the Government of the Czech Republic', in,28th session; Consideration of Reports Submitted by State Parties in Accordance with Article 16 ICESCR 2002).

reality (for example, the right to property). This argument undermines assertions that have been put forward by some constitution drafters who claimed that negligence of socio-economic rights in democratic constitutions would give a green light to the legislators to reduce, or even to ignore the granting of social benefits. In fact, even if there is the assumption that the affection to the communist/socialistic social rights was deeply rooted in the societies, it does not exclude the fact in favour of the constitutionalisation of these rights in a new democratic constitution. It could have been equally claimed that the expectation would otherwise shift first of all to the legislator, and second to the performance of the Constitutional Court.[169] Moreover, some have affirmed that many social and economic rights, even if not present in the Constitution, would oblige legislators to undertake adequate steps to guarantee these rights.[170]

Some members of the Constitutional Commission in Poland were inclined to arrange the power of judicial review in line with the American model. Ultimately, a solution closer to the European continental tradition prevailed and a constitutional court, inspired by the German model, was created. The question remained, however, how to define the function of the individual constitutional complaint. It was feared that complaints by private persons challenging the constitutionality of a piece of legislation would flood the Tribunal and thus undermine the whole institution of judicial review.[171] Indirectly, the choice of the form of judicial review would in some way influence the controversy over whether the constitutional text should be considered as a symbolic or as a legal text. The latter solution, closer to the American constitutional tradition, implies that the constitution must primarily include provisions that courts could enforce without upsetting the proper balance of power among the branches of the government.

3.3.2 Ombudsmen- Bringing Constitution Closer to the Individual

Human rights promotion and protection in a state is conducted by different means depending upon the type of institution responsible for enforcement and implementation of fundamental rights. The allocation of jurisdiction between human rights institutions may be divided into two main categories of bodies responsible for human rights protection and promotion.

169 The Hungarian Constitutional Court provides the example of the latter situation. Namely, the Court has given expression to the popular expectations in its judgements on social rights.

170 Herman Schwartz, *In Defence of Aiming High*, Fall East European Constitutional Review, 1992.

171 Andrzej Rapaczyński, *Constitutional Politics in Poland...*, p.610.

Historically, this mandate has been assigned to an independent judiciary and constitutional courts. The concept of non-judiciary protection of human rights arose from the significant development of an idea of "detaching" fundamental rights protection from the influence of a state. The non-judiciary protection is not only carried out by independent institutions such as national or international NGOs. Additionally, the role is being undertaken more and more often by the national human rights institutions, which are neither executive, nor judicial or legislative bodies; instead they are situated between the government and civil society sphere.

The idea of national human rights institutions, although established at national levels, has been defined in the United Nations framework and has led to the adoption of the Paris Principles.[172] National human rights institutions (NHRIs) are set up either by legislation or by constitution, with a goal to improve human rights protection and promotion in a given state. They differ in numbers, names and mandates assigned to their activities, depending on each state's arbitrary decision on how to set up its own system of fundamental rights protection and promotion. The framework laid down in the Paris Principles defines national institutions as bodies which shall be given as broad mandate as possible with emphasis on the national implementation of international human rights standards. They shall fulfil a range of responsibilities in relation to the government, the parliament, or other competent bodies. That is, they should advise theses bodies, submit opinions, recommendations, proposals and reports on any matter concerning human rights or any situation of violation of human rights. The central characteristics of an NHRI are its independence and pluralist representation of the civil society. An NHRI shall increase public awareness of human rights through information, education and media. It may, but does not have to be authorized to consider individual complaints.

When comparing the institutional design of non-judicial human rights systems in Poland, the Czech Republic and Slovakia, an obvious difference becomes apparent at the first glance. Each of the three countries has a different set

172 The Paris Principles are guidelines which provide for a comprehensive series of recommendations on the competences, responsibilities, composition, status and functions of national human rights institutions, but not every national institution fully complies with all of these standards. They were defined at the International Workshop on National Institutions for the Promotion and Protection of Human Rights, Paris 7-9 October 1991, E/CN.4/1992/43 of 16 December 1991. The principles were further endorsed by the United Nations Commission on Human Rights in Resolution 1992/54, 1992, and by the General Assembly in its resolution A/RES/48/134, of 20 December 1993.

of institutions active within the field of the promotion and protection of human rights. In general, Poland has one institution responsible for the general promotion and protection of human rights, which is the Ombudsman, who under Polish legislation is called the Commissioner for Civil Rights Protection.[173] Although, the English translation of the Commissioner's full title suggests that the Polish Ombudsman only focuses on civil rights, this is not the case. The Commissioner is given a wide human rights mandate, which also covers social and economic rights monitoring.

Slovakia has accepted a dual system of human rights institutions. Besides the Ombudsman (the Public Defender of Rights), [174] Slovakia has also set up the Slovak National Centre for Human Rights (SNCHR) as a NHRI. The Centre monitors and assesses the respect for human rights standards in the country, conducts research, education activities, and increases public awareness of human rights in general. It therefore fulfils many functions assigned to an NHRI, but it is not equipped with any particular competences that might play a significant role in protection or promotion of any of the constitutional human rights. The 2005 report of the SNSHR shows, however, that the activity of the Centre within the field of social rights was focused on education, especially concerning the principle of equal treatment and non-discrimination of certain categories of citizens. A number of seminars was organised by the Centre for elected representatives and employees of local-government administration. The practical dimension was to "inform the public (target groups) about the need to take measures to prevent from discrimination, and to explain the means of legal protection, including the option of proceedings before the court in the matters of violation of the principle of equal treatment" when the cases of "discrimination in the access to allowances and services of social security, health care, education, providing goods and services, and in legal employment and similar legal relations".[175]

The Czech Republic's system comprises three different bodies. The Czech triplet of non-judicial human rights bodies, which composes a single institutional structure, carries out the functions of an NHRI to a considerable degree. Nevertheless, it does not fully meet international standards leaving the gaps and

173 The Office of the Commissioner for Civil Rights Protection in Poland has been created by the Act on the Commissioner for Civil Rights Protection, 15 July 1987.

174 Position created by Act no. 564/2001 Coll. on the Public Defender of Rights.

175 For details see: 2005 Annual Report on Activities of the Slovak National Centre for Human Rights. The Report may be found at: www.snslp.sk/rs/snslp_rs.nsf/0/B76DD2FB0C07822CC1257237004D9666?OpenDocument

shortcomings in the systemic, independent monitoring of human rights at the national level. Apart from the classic parliamentary ombudsman,[176] the non-judicial system of protection and promotion of human rights is composed of the government official (the Commissioner for Human Rights), and the advisory council of the government (the Human Rights Council). The ambiguity in a clear separation of tasks and responsibilities of the Commissioner and the Council triggers a concern over the lack of independent mechanisms for the practical implementation of human rights monitoring.[177] Both, the Human Rights Commissioner and the Human Rights Council co-ordinate government activities within the field of human rights and are affiliated to the Government Office. Since the Secretariat of the Human Rights Council is a sub-unit of the Human Rights Department of the Government Office, of which in turn the Commissioner is a director, the Human Rights Council although defined as the government's permanent consultative body, is a *de facto* advisory body to the Human Rights Commissioner. Moreover, the Council besides its advisory functions is assigned with some of the tasks of the executive, such as to prepare strategies and concrete measures. The clear picture of the Commissioner and the Council's functions is blurred by the fact that both do not have any statutory basis.[178] Therefore, even when examining the principle of plural representation,[179] which according to the Paris Principles is one of the characteristics of NHRI, its structure is not representative. This feature is not guaranteed through legitimate procedures. According to the Statute of the Council, it may establish standing

176 The post of the Public Defender of Rights in the Czech Republic was created by Act no. 349/1999 Coll. on the Public Defender of Rights.

177 See i.e. Concluding Observations of the Human Rights Committee: Czech Republic, CCPR/CO/72/CZE, 27 August 2001, Concluding Observations of the Committee on Economic, Social and Cultural Rights: Czech Republic, E/C.12/1 Add.76, 5 June 2002.

178 The Human Rights Council and the Human Rights Commissioner were established by a government decree of December 9, 1998 No.809. It means that both the Council as well as the post of the Commissioner may be changed at any time by a single government decree. Yet, such a situation is unlikely for the sake of national considerations and international consequences.

179 It seems that the question of pluralism within the Human Rights Council is nevertheless disputable. Even though the Council is composed of the representatives of the executive at the deputy minister level, and the representatives of the civil society (*i.e.* associations' representatives, personalities in public life, independent experts), the representation is not equal. Moreover, a principle of the balance of interests and powers on which the Council's composition is based is infringed upon by the overrepresentation and status of public officials. The fact that they enjoy voting rights brings about doubt over what kind of added value stems from the fact that the government is being advised by the public officials.

Committees, among which there is a Committee for Economic, Social and Cultural rights (*Výbor pro hospodářská, sociální a kulturní práva*). Each Committee may invite an external expert (*spolupracovnik*) to work in the Committee. The competences of Committees are so broadly defined that they do not refer to the specific matters of the Committee's competence.[180] This argument, however, may not shade the activities of the Council within the field of social rights. For example, it took the decision of 19 June 2006 which addresses the issue of social inclusion and the measures to be adopted in order to counteract it (*Usnesení Rady vlády ČR pro lidská práva ze dne 9. června 2006 k problematice bydlení osob ohrožených sociálním vyloučením).*[181]

Turning to the question of powers that the aforementioned institutions have with regard to the judicial system, it is evident that only Ombudsmen are assigned with such kinds of competences that allow them to potentially enter into a more or less developed relationship with the courts, and especially with the constitutional courts. In the scholarly debate, there are two roles of Ombudsmen identified with respect to the varying operational methods and objectives. Firstly, the Ombudsmen are seen as authorities that provide redress for individual grievances, and secondly, they are concerned with improving administrative practices. Thus, the ideal type of the Ombudsmen would combine the function of an instrument of redress, with the function of quality control.[182] This implies, consequently, that turning to a court becomes an effective tool the Ombudsman may be equipped with in order to protect the rights of the individual.

Given his greater authority, the Polish Commissioner for Civil Rights must be distinguished from his Czech and Slovak counterparts. Besides having the power to bring an action against individual and general acts to the Constitutional Tribunal, administrative courts and common courts, the Polish Ombudsman has the right to intervene in the conduct and activities of the government and local government's organs. Conversely, the Czech and the Slovak Ombudsmen are not entitled to appeal against acts and actions (or inactions) of public organs. Their competence is limited to addressing recommendations to adequate organs; that is their competence is limited to filing a petition to those institutions (or to their superior organs) that have infringed the law, and to request that the particular authorities change their policies. However, such an action does not have the

---

180 See: Article 6(4) of the Statute of the Government Council for Human Rights.

181 To be found on the website of the Czech government: www.vlada.cz

182 M. Senevirante, *Ombudsmen. Public Services and Administrative Justice*, Butterworths, LexisNexis, 2002, p. 17.

force of law.[183] If an action undertaken by the Ombudsman is not effective in the way that the institutions are unwilling to respond to the Ombudsman's claims, nor are they willing to take upon themselves the challenged provisions, the Ombudsmen may refer the case to the constitutional court. During the proceedings, the Ombudsmen may ask the constitutional court to indicate when the validity of a challenged provision or of the act will expire. Moreover, both Czech and Slovak Ombudsmen may submit a proposal for the annulment of an administrative provision.[184] In the case of Poland such a possibility does not exist, since the adjudication of the Polish Constitutional Tribunal on constitutional complaints is limited, in a way that it refers only to the legal provision on which the individual judgment or decision is based.[185]

The Polish Commissioner, however, has a unique power which allows him/her to support the constitutional complaint of a citizen and may support the citizen's argumentation in front of the Constitutional Tribunal. The controversy in respect of this competence revolves around the fact that it is unclear whether the Ombudsman can indicate different constitutional provisions than those indicated by the applicant. Recent developments in the Polish constitutional jurisprudence tend to enable the Ombudsman to widen the scope of the referred constitutional principles, as long as they concern fundamental rights and freedoms. It may not be forgotten, however, that the admissibility of the Ombudsman's appeal is conditioned upon finding a violation of constitutional freedoms and human rights. Moreover, the Ombudsman intervenes only in those cases where he/she sees the citizen without the capability to defend him/herself, or when the case may either set a precedent or may have a bearing on future similar cases.

All things considered, the result of the interaction between the Ombudsmen and the constitutional courts in the three presented countries brings the conclusion that competences to refer to the constitutional courts in one way or another contribute to the safeguarding and development of the democratic process. The facilities provided for by the Ombudsmen in bringing justice closer to the citizens, in the way that they facilitate the access to courts, are mainly due to easy access to the Ombudsperson, a broad spectrum of problems which may be addressed by his/her office, and the fact that the consultation or lodging an appeal to an Ombudsman is free of charge. Protection and promotion of the rule of law and of fundamental rights, as well as an attempt to assure the efficiency and proficiency of judicial decisions, is a common ground upon which the role of courts

183 J. Świątkiewicz, *Rzecznik Praw Obywatelskich a sądownictwo administracyjne po reformie*, Biuro Rzecznika Praw Obywatelskich, 2004, p.7.

184 Czech Republic - Law No. 182/1993 Coll. On the Constitutional Court, Section 64(2).

185 Article 79 and Article section 5 of the Polish Constitution.

and NHRIs overlap. They differ, nevertheless, in their approach to dispute resolution. It is often acknowledged that only the courts make legally binding decisions. They also differ in a scope of activity – the court's function is to ensure adherence to legality, while non-judicial institutions promote the idea of good governance, which in the case of safeguarding fair and transparent social policies consequential to the constitutional guarantees, remains an important issue to be ensured by the human rights institutions. Proceedings that the Ombudsman can launch before the constitutional court give an opportunity to undertake actions to improve the judicial system, and to bring the conformity and clarity of the law. The cooperation and the fact that the Ombudsman and constitutional courts complement one another, leads to strengthening the efficiency of the protection system of fundamental rights and freedoms. Hence, the review of the extent and limitations of NHRIs' interactions within the constitutional courts, shows clearly that the full picture of the state's institutional framework, the one which includes such bodies as Ombudsmen, has a significant bearing on the performance in human rights implementation and enforcement at the national level. It may also influence national human rights agendas over a long period of time.

3.3.3 Other Constitutional Bodies- Special Control Actors

The realisation of the statutory obligations of the state within the social policies is controlled by specialized control actors. The performances of these organs need to be seen in the perspective of the specificity of the Polish, Czech and Slovak history; more precisely, within the context of democratic transformation, which has largely influenced economic changes in the 1990s. On the one hand, the transformation processes created new opportunities to manage public spending allocated for the protection of the most indigent people. On the other hand, however, it fostered possibilities for pathologies within the institutions, especially on the local community level, where the accessibility to public spending resources has not always been well protected, which is what in turn has led to the spread of corruption. Yet, democracy requires a system of checks and balances within its institutional system. Therefore, institutions such as the specialized control organs constitute a significant link in the final chain within social policy implementation and conduct.

Supreme Audit Institutions (SAIs), such as the Polish Supreme Chamber of Control[186] and Supreme Audit Offices in the case of the Czech Republic[187] and Slovakia,[188] play important roles within the institutional mechanisms of the democratic state. Acting within the wider area of democratic politics and administration, they are given a high level of independence, which is what allows them to secure public accountability for the probity and legality of public spending, as well as the efficiency and effectiveness of the national economy.[189] They are the national bodies that have the power to hold other public organisations accountable for the use of public funds and for their performance. It is particularly interesting to analyse the scope of duties and responsibilities the control organs have been equipped with, as well as to question what evidence these organs offer as to the quality and effectiveness of their activities in the protection and promotion of socio-economic rights.

The general observation of activities of the Polish, Czech and Slovak SAIs leads to the conclusion that within the priority directions and main areas of audit research, issues concerning observance of socio-economic rights constitute a significant part of the overall activities of the Offices.[190] The questions over the performance of state bodies within the field of health protection and promotion, for example, were well placed within the audit activities conducted by Polish and Czech SAIs in the last two years.[191] Further, the issue of the restructurisation

186 Legal regulations for the Polish *Najwyższa Izba Kontroli* (NIK) are enshrined in Chapter IX of the Constitution, Act of 23 December 1994, on the Supreme Chamber of Control, and Regulation of the President of the Supreme Chamber of Control of March 1st, 1995 on Audit Proceedings.

187 The legal basis for the Czech's *Nejvyšší Kontrolní Úřad* (NKÚ) is laid down in Chapter V of the Constitution and by Act No.166/1993 Coll., of May 20th, 1993.

188 The legal basis for the Slovak *Nejvyšší Kontrolní Úřad* (NKÚ) is laid down in Arts.60-63 of the Constitution and Act No. 39 of the National Council of the Slovak Republic of January 19, 1993.

189 Ch. Pollitt, H. Summa, *Reflexive Watchdogs? How Supreme Audit Institutions Account for Themselves*, Public Administration, No. 75, 1997, p.313.

190 The available documents used in this analysis differ significantly in their extent and nature. For the activities of the Polish Supreme Chamber of Control an Activity Report for the year 2005 has been used. For the same analysis of the performance of the Czech Supreme Audit Office only priority points could have been extracted from the Audit Plan and some of the information from press releases of the conducted audit in 2006. There is already a discrepancy over the time periods of the analyzed activities. In the case of the Slovak Supreme Audit Office a secondary source was helpful.

191 The Annual Report 2005 (#130/2006) of the Polish Supreme Chamber of Control (from now: the Annual Report 2005 of NIK), available at www.nik.gov.pl/dzialalnosc_en.php and Press Release of 8 March 2007 of the Czech NKÚ, *Ministry of Healthcare did not control the teaching hospitals development grant-in-aid*, www.nku.cz/scripts/detail.asp?id=1448.

of the economy has been given a high priority in all three institutions.[192] Polish and Slovak Supreme Audit Institutions have conducted audits of financial management of the companies and enterprises and of their financial commitments, in which the State Treasury and agencies hold shares.[193] Interestingly, there are examples of cooperation between the SAIs consisting of the performance of parallel audits of jointly selected areas. The Regional Branch of the NIK began to cooperate with the Slovak NKÚ in the control of the functioning of national parks with regard to sustainable use and restoration of natural resources.[194]

192 Here controls usually included audits of systems of subsidies and granting public aid in the context of the EU requirements, as well as audits of activity of public administration bodies related to raising the European Union's structural funds.

193 For comparison see: the Annual Report 2005 of NIK and a survey conducted in December 2005 by the National Audit Office of the United Kingdom (NAO) available at www.nao.org.uk/publications/state_audit/State_Audit_Book.pdf.

194 The Annual Report 2005 of NIK, p.21.

Chapter 4
Substantial Change in The Meaning of Socio-Economic Rights

4.1 Modality of Rights' Constitutional Formulation

The modality in which social and economic rights are formulated in constitutions, here understood as an exact formulation of a given right, is not only a classical categorisation of rights as justiciable versus non-justiciable, or as claim rights versus principles; it is also a matter of the narrative that is inherent to the wording of a given right.[195] By introducing the term *modality* greater attention is being paid to the importance that the constitution-building process has on the future understanding of any particular right. It is useful therefore to try to uncover whether discussions held on the meaning, scope and objective of a given right are of consequence when it comes to deciding on the intensity of and ways in which the efficacy is given to that right in the process of constitutional adjudication.

As already mentioned, the substantial change that social and economic rights have gained once they have been inscribed in new democratic constitutions, has brought about numerous debates over justiciability and judicial enforcement, or at least the awareness of the existent ambiguity of constitutional formulation of these rights within constitutional debates in Central and Eastern Europe. It was not only the way in which social and economic rights were enshrined in the constitutions of the researched countries that was important, but most importantly, the way in which constitutional courts were given competence to deal with the issue of jus-

195 I base this argument on the idea of historical narratives in constitutional adjudication elaborated by Renáta Uitz in her book Constitutions, Courts and History (see: Renáta Uitz, *Constitutions, Courts and History*, CEU Press, 2005. I also add, however, an idea that it is the constitution-building moment that frames the understanding of a given right.

ticiability of social and economic rights in their jurisprudence. The Constitutional Courts' preference to either base a judgment or a decision solely on constitutional principles (such as the principle of social state), or on a specific right (if existent), or eventually on a clear linkage of principles and rights (in case of socio-economic rights considered as mutually enforcing), brings the argument back to the original point about a manner in which a given right is understood depending on the modality of its constitutional formulation.

The complexities of the two main elements constitute therefore a semantic for social and economic rights in Central Eastern European constitutions. These are the institutional and substantive reforms within the constitutional framework of socio-economic formulation on one hand, and on the other the role of constitutional courts therein.

4.1.1 Constitutionalisation of Socio-Economic Rights

Constitutional debates that accompanied the 1990s' democratisation processes in Central and Eastern Europe concentrated on two main aspects: the justiciability and state's capacity to materialize social and economic constitutional rights into effective policies. Apart from political issue as to whether to include social and economic rights within new democratic constitutions or not, the enforcement of these rights was discussed. It appears that, especially in the period of transition to democracy, it was essential to create mechanisms of implementation and more importantly of judicial enforcement of social and economic rights. Still, the general problem of whether to assign constitutional justiciability to all social and economic rights remains debatable in the constitutional theory for a number of reasons. The analysis of legal, political, economic and moral justifications for the constitutional justiciability of social and economic rights fully reviews fundamental disputes in the approach to socio-economic rights. In each of these crucial spheres socio-economic guarantees are either justified or rejected, which shows the complex nature of these rights. On the other hand, the debate opens up the question of the availability of resources needed for the enforcement of these constitutional rights by the state. The most commonly shared opinion revolves around the fact that it is meaningless to provide for socio-economic rights without the resources to ensure their protection. There is a strong tendency in academia, and among many practitioners, to present social and economic rights as guiding principles for the state and its institutions, thus limiting their justiciability and attributing them at most a "judicially cognisable" character.

Within this dual distinction of constitutional social and economic rights, that emphasises notions of their justiciability and *concretisation* into effective policies, there are still two other fundamental issues. Namely, the relationship between socio-economic and civil-political rights followed by consideration over their positive versus negative nature, and on the other hand as "minimal" versus "strong" use of the socio-economic rights in the process of their enforcement in constitutional judicial review.[196] Secondly, in the evolution of the democratisation and constitutionalisation processes in Central Eastern Europe, the legitimacy of democratic foundations in the countries of democratic transformation (social protection and economic rights promotion included), was a recurrent question not only in political debates but also in the scholarly discourse.

The credibility of constitution-building process was sometimes questioned, be it either democratic legitimacy of constitution framers which was disputed or the way in which the constitution itself has been enacted (timing, openness and length of discussions, etc.). This leads to further elaboration over the question of the legitimisation of social and economic rights in the specific context of their placement in democratic constitutions of post-communist countries - this being a perspective for a general debate on the legitimacy of post-communist democratic regimes and their constitutional foundations in general. In order to clarify this problem, it is advisable to trace not only the pedigree of socio-economic constitutional provisions, but also the differences in terms of their justiciability depending on their scope- whether they are enclosed in the form of brief statements or broad recitations of fundamental political principles. The moment when the drafters decide whether or not to inscribe social and economic rights in the constitution, the short- and long- term political interests need to be balanced. The political culture and the agreed way in which the drafters proceed when deciding upon the scope of socio-economic provisions influences the character and provides for a conventional definition of these rights. Despite the prevailing moral component that characterises their nature, social and economic rights also lend themselves to the purpose of the institutional design of the state. Socio-economic constitutional rights not only form the type of relations between state authorities and individuals, but also they influence intra-institutional relations. On the other hand however, these rights by themselves do not fill the system with the meaning. They are one among many other tools which democracy builders may use in order to enhance democratic institutional behaviours.

One of the characteristic features of the post-communist countries is the predominance of state authorities over the role and activity of civil society. It was often the case that the impulse for democratic change came from the bot-

196 The latter term is used by Sadurski, see: Wojciech Sadurski, *Ibid.*, p.172.

tom-up, thus activating different social groups to action, allocating the sense of responsibility to social actors and consequently contributing to the formation of the civil society. This is at least the theory. The practice is often far from ideal and it discloses an attempt to verbalise the high expectations for improvement of living and working conditions. By the same token, the process of democratisation favoured popular expectations for the constitutionalisation of social and economic rights, what the constitutional frameworks had to face and take into account.

4.1.2 Justiciability and Constitutional Courts

Regardless of constitutional fixation the judicial enforcement of socio-economic rights has to be performed on different levels and by different means. The mode and scope of constitutional formulation require appropriate judicial techniques. Moreover, constitutional justiciablity and the role of constitutional courts therein results in concrete consequences. It is widely accepted that constitutional courts' decisions influence the policy goals of the state and sometimes even shape the rulings of the respective policies. Whether it is a positive or a negative mechanism, is debatable. It largely depends on the extent and direction to which the court directs the resultant policy, and to which the legislator/government is ready to consider the court's judgements. Therefore, it is right to underline the significance and controversies that the finality of constitutional courts' decisions bring within a democratic setting.[197] The tension between electorally accountable bodies and the judiciary in the allocation of authority when policies are decided remains troublesome, at least with the extent to which such arguments as legitimacy, capacity and expertise are being raised.[198] An assessment of constitutional justiciability, is therefore concerned with the division of socio-economic rights into those which are directly enforceable in the constitution or those whose judicial enforceability is dependent on legislative discretion. Such consideration does not have any direct transposition over the question of socio-economic rights' justiciability nor on their judicial enforceability at the statutory level. Constitutional enforceability is a way by which certain rights are strength-

197 A comprehensive explanation of the idea of the "last word" has been presented by Thomas Nagel. Especially meaningful is an affirmation of difficulty in finding the last word in disputes which touch upon ethical issues and concern the objectivity of any form of ideological background. See: Thomas Nagel, *The Last Word*, Oxford University Press, 1997.

198 For an in depth study on this issue in context of CEE countries see: Wojciech Sadurski, *Postcommunist Constitutional Courts in Search of Political Legitimacy*, EUI Working Paper LAW No. 2001/11, Florence, 2001.

ened and some are assigned to the highest judicial considerations, having a bearing on a state's policies through the constitutional review. The resultant categorisation of social and economic rights, based on the differences in the judicial enforcement, does not automatically imply any form of hierarchy on these rights. Moreover, the practice shows that the leading role of constitutional courts in adjudication on socio-economic matters has a positive effect on the realisation of social and economic rights derived from the constitution. The principle of fairness in adjudication on social and economic matters gives a mandate to courts when determining whether the state is complying with its obligations of progressive implementation, in evaluating whether measures were adopted to address the problem areas and whether such measures were reasonable, both in their conception and implementation. Hence, the differentiation between claim or entitlement, resultant rights and principled state guidelines, serves to recognize the actual *status quo* of socio-economic constitutional provisions and underline the diverging means of their judicial enforcement.

4.2 Substantial Change of Socio-Economic Rights' Meaning

The ideology of communist regimes placed several constraints on the elaboration of social and economic rights in new democratic constitutions. The central control over economic processes and the lack of judicial mechanisms for the protection and promotion of constitutionally guaranteed social and economic rights have not only undermined the effectiveness of the operation of markets, but have also stripped their meaning, degrading socio-economic provisions to the empty promises under the full interpretation of the communist party.

Although, as suggested in the introduction, there were common basic factors in the communist economic regimes of Central Eastern European countries, based on Marxist rhetoric. There were also some differences in the way these factors functioned in each country. This, indeed, results from the way in which internal policies were conducted, the position the national Communist Party succeeded to maintain, and the general independence from the Kremlin dictatorship. With the democratic changes the old slogans and fundamental institutions of the communist order- such as monopoly of power of the communist party, omnipresent bureaucracy, state ownership of means of production, and centrally administered economy- were widely contested. At a certain point it became obvious that economic reforms and creation of a "law-based society" or a "civil society" was a must, or rather a reality which would not have been contested any longer. In general, there was a strong need to introduce a new constitutional order based on principles of the rule of law, political accountability to the people, the legitimacy of political opposition. At the same time transition to the market economy was equally important and desired.

The societal acceptance of the economic reforms, connected with hazards of radical reforms causing the loss of security and stability that the old system had guaranteed, became one of the most pertinent issues for the reformers. Would the citizens of the socialist countries, whose minds were stirred by the propaganda rhetoric insisting on a simple recognition that socialism is "good" and that capitalism is "bad", agree to sacrifice and to contribute to the well-being of the society as a whole, renouncing *ipso facto* the entitlements and privileges that the communist, and later socialist, state had guaranteed? Would the change of the mentality of citizens keep up with the reform spirit? With the previous in mind, wealth-creating activities or an idea of the entrepreneurial push, linked to a requirement to take up individual responsibility thus diminishing the role of the state in welfare-provisions, could not have been expected to be really accepted or valued by many. Some scholars point to the prevailing preference for the security of a known system, versus the unpredictable consequences of change.[199] The long-lived socialist system adjusted the minds of many people to claim-based attitudes, acceptance of corruptive behaviours, hampering in this way the appreciation for individual responsibilities protected by real and feasible rights.

The conceptualisation of constitutional principles of liberty and equality as a fundamental basis proving tight reciprocity between social and economic duties the individuals owe to the community, and the duties the community owes to the individuals, has proven to be a complex challenge with regard to Central Eastern European systems. The values of constitutionalism, the rule of law, and the protection of rights were not well grounded at the time the constitutional debates were held. Beyond central concerns such as "a minimalist tradition of treating a constitution as a purely decorative instrument", or "fundamental notions of constitutionalism and the rule of law hav[ing] a weak hold upon the collective consciousness", the constitutional debates revolved around justiciability, judicial enforcement and the scope on social and economic provisions.[200] With regard to the communist heritage and challenges of democratisation many arguments have

199 Robert W. Campbell, *The Socialist Economies in Transition*, Indiana University Press, 1991.

200 Wojciech Sadurski, *Constitutional Courts in the Process of Articulating Constitutional Rights...*, p.13.

been evoked both in favour and against the implementation of social and economic provisions in the. As a result, the Czech Charter of Fundamental Rights and Basic Freedoms, for example, formulates the employment entitlements stating that the working conditions should be "satisfactory" with details to be further set by a separate law. In the Slovak Constitution the idea is developed by enumerating seven categories of entitlements, including, for instance the setting of a maximum number of working hours, a reasonable rest time after work and a minimum amount of paid vacation. Such extensive wording may be seen as a broadening of the general provision which consequently leads to a blurring of its meaning. A positive interpretation of the constitutional provision in the constitutional act itself, which includes a detailed scope of interpretation, apart from being distorted, is widely contested.[201] The strengthening of economic and social rights in this case is seen as making the said rights practical as opposed to theoretical. An interesting view point was presented, for example, by at that time soon to-be Polish prime minister Hanna Suchocka in the 1990s during the debates over constitutional provisions organized by the Poznan Human Rights Centre. Suchocka claimed that the distinctive features of social and economic rights are well reflected when considering the differences between social security (*ubezpieczenie społeczne*) and social service (*pomoc społeczna*). The former is guaranteed by a system of welfare provisions protecting the citizens from defined but incidental risks (*zabepieczenie społeczne*). There is therefore a need to perceive social and economic rights as complementary attitudes of individuals who have a choice and a need to enjoy specific rights, and the state has a duty to guarantee these rights. The role of the state is consequently seen as subsidiary in relation to the competences the individuals must undertake to enjoy the given right.[202]

During communist period, as well as in the State of real socialism (*państwo realnego socjalizmu*), the law was used as an instrument for controlling social processes. The axiology of law was mainly reduced to its political functions. As a consequence law was instrumentally used to steer political processes in their institutional dimension. The role of the Communist Party was prevalent, as the attention was being brought on the development of the institutions that served the ideology of the real socialism doctrine. The social function of law was lim-

201 For more details see: E. Stein, *Czecho/Slovakia. Ethnic Conflict, Constitutional Fissure...*, p.279-280.

202 For more details see: Hanna Suchocka, *Zakres i sposób regulacji praw ekonomicznych, socjalnych i kulturalnych a przyszłej konstytucji.*, in: Zdzisław Kędzia (ed.), *Prawa, wolności i obowiązki człowieka i obywatela*, 1990.

ited to the state's interest, such as the building of socialism, protection and promotion of socialistic achievements of the working class (Polish: *lud pracujący*, Czech: *pracujúci ľud*), etc. The constitution was a propaganda manifesto, which did not address the actual status of an individual nor did it define a relationship between state and individual. The value of the constitution of the state of socialism was illusory as it did not guarantee rights or freedoms provided for in its text. There were no enforcement mechanisms that would allow individuals to claim and assert their constitutional rights. The constitutional rights were therefore mock and delusive, especially when compared to the role that constitutional rights play in the constitutions embedded in democratic values. In this case, democratic constitutional principles necessitate that limits of state power are defined and that the relationship between a state its institutions and individuals are determined. Accordingly the law acts as a means for the protection of individual rights and freedoms, it serves as a communication tool both between individuals and their representatives who embody the function of the state powers, as well as it is a communication tool between various state actors.

Chapter 5
Constitutional Socio-Economic Jurisprudence in Selected Matters

5.1 Right to Health Care

Health as a human right was first addressed by the World Health Organisation (WHO) Constitution signed in 1946. Ever since that time "the enjoyment of the highest attainable standard of health [understood as] one of the fundamental rights of every human beings"[203] have been discussed in reference to the political and legal dimensions both on international and domestic/constitutional scenes. The initial problem was to define what exactly the right to "the highest attainable standard to health" meant. It is worth noting here, that two years after it was adopted in the Universal Declaration of Human Rights (UDHR), which referred to "the right to a standard of living adequate for health and well-being"[204] of each individual. It was not until 1961, however, when the right to the protection of health was recognised by the European Social Charter[205] (ESC), and later in 1966 when the Covenant on Economic, Social and Cultural Rights[206] (ICESCR) formulated the right to health as an autonomous right. This historical snap-shot of the formulation of the right to health reflects the essence of debates over its legal meaning, and most of all, over its legal contents. In brief, the international community has gone through the formulation of a de-

---

203 Preamble to the Constitution of the Word Health Organisation. World Health Organisation. (1946).

204 Article 25(1) of the Universal Declaration of Human Rights. United Nations General Assembly. (1948).

205 Article 11 of the European Social Charter. ETS No. 035. (1961). Entered into force on 26 February 1965, then revised in Strasbourg on 3 May 1996, and entered into force on 1 July 1999.

206 Article 12 of the International Covenant on Economic, Social and Cultural Rights. (1966).. The ICESCR entered into force on 3 January 1976.

claration to guarantee the "highest attainable standard" to the protection of health as a right in itself. Yet, this debate over the denotation and subject of the right to health has deeper roots.

Looking at the discussions on the modern concept of health, and consequently on the right to health, it is apparent that this notion is not uniform, and it manifests itself in at least two different, but concomitant expressions. The concept of health is most commonly derived from two related disciplines: that of medicine and that of public health.[207] Reducing the problem to a single question, the former relates to medical considerations over an individual's physical or mental illness and disability, while the latter concerns deliberations over systemic health care issues. To the contrary, the expression of the right to health, as a general concept, takes the form of both an individual and social right. It is a common misconception of legal literature, however, which reduces it to either individual right to health (protection) or to social right to health care. Despite this common oversimplification, most legal documents introduce a conceptual differentiation between these two expressions.[208]

Despite being expressed in various international treaties, the right to health is also guaranteed, in one form or another, in a number of national European constitutions.[209] Nevertheless, the realisation of the right to health takes on different dimensions and consequences not only because its constitutional formulation varies, but also because it acquires different meaning throughout constitutional jurisprudence. However, regardless of its diverse constitutional formulation and differences in its legal structure, the right to health care seems to converge on the consequences of the limitations that have been assigned to its realisation within various legal systems.[210] Needless to say, even if not found within the text of a constitution, this right is placed instead within national health legislation, and, so may be derived from national jurisprudence.

---

207 Jonathan M. Mann et al., *Health and Human Rights*, Health and Human Rights, No.1, 1994, p.8-9.

208 Aart Hendriks, *The Right to Health in National and International Jurisprudence*, European Journal of Health Law, No. 5, 1998.

209 From among 46 State Parties of the Council of Europe, only a few Constitutions do not explicitly mention the right to health protection/care.

210 André Den Exter, Bert Hermans, *Constitutional Rights to Health Care: The Consequences of Placing limits to the Right to Health Care in several Western and Eastern European Countries*, European Journal of Health Law, No.5, 1998. By comparing legal and health policy developments in Italy, the Netherlands, the United Kingdom, Poland and Hungary, Den Exter and Hermans suggest that the convergence point largely concerns the interpretation of the right to health care by national (constitutional) courts.

Constitutions of Poland, the Czech Republic and Slovakia formally distinguish the right to the protection of health,[211] from the right to health care services. Notwithstanding the very similar linguistic formulations of the right to the protection of health, it is interesting to see that the three Courts do not interpret the right to protection to health in the same way. It may seem that the distinction lies in the textual formulation of the constitutional articles. In the case of the Polish Constitution the right to health is formulated in five paragraphs, each of which has been separately dealt with by the Constitutional Tribunal. At the same time, the Tribunal referred to the right to health care with a more systemic interpretation, emphasizing its scope and the resulting obligation of the state to provide health services. This is why the Polish Constitutional Tribunal used a wide interpretation of the right to the protection of health considering it as a fundamental human right. On the other hand, the Czech and Slovak expression of the right to health (in general terms) is captured in single paragraph-formulation, which anticipates a joint interpretation of this part of the right with its remaining component, that is the right to medical care. Notwithstanding, different approaches of the courts, they all interpret the right to the protection of health in relatively broad terms. Not only because this right is constitutionally guaranteed to everybody, as opposed to the right to health care, which is given to citizens only. But also because the right to the protection of health is interpreted by the Constitutional Courts as a right to health in general.

Although the comparison of the Polish, Czech and Slovak understanding of the right to the protection of health, together with the health care systems, and the legal environments in which these systems operate unveil differences, the three countries face the same problem of limited resources for health care juxtaposed with the legal right of patients to such care. This problem, even though of a political nature, has a deep impact on constitutional jurisprudence.

5.1.1 Health as Individual Constitutional Right

Despite recognition of the right to health as a human right, much remains unsettled with respect to its materialisation. It is largely because of the controversy and lack of clarity about the nature, scope and the normative meaning of this right. As it has been argued above, the right to health takes on various aspects, depending on its formulation and the understanding assigned to it by various

211 Article 68, prara.1 of the Polish Constitution (*prawo do ochrony zdrowia*), Article 31 of the Czech Charter on Fundamental Rights and Basic Freedoms (*právo na ochranu zdraví*), and Article 40 of the Slovak Constitution (*právo na ochranu zdravia*).

actors, both on an international and national level, who are responsible for its implementation, protection and promotion. Accordingly, the right to health in general terms manifests itself as an individual right, and as a social right.

The right to health as an individual right is most commonly referred to as a right to the promotion or protection of health. It is not, however, connected to the design and function of a health care system, but a special emphasis is placed in this respect on the ontological aspect of the right to health, which is that of the integrity of a human person. Such a context entails an obligation to protection of the human body and personal integrity. It is therefore apparent that in this understanding the right to health protection is inherently consistent with the principle of human dignity. Consequently, once the innate and inalienable dignity of a human person is considered to be a constituent part of the right to health protection, the State and its organs have a duty to respect and protect this fundamental human right. As far as the adjudication on health protection, the principle of human dignity became a primary basis for judicial decisions. Various courts more or less explicitly acknowledge that States are required to ensure at least a minimum level of health protection and (equal) access to health services, through the satisfaction of basic human needs. This means that the right to the protection of health is treated as a substantive right of an individual person to have his/her health protected. The content of this right may be therefore described as the function of a consequence, which is that the innate and undeniable human dignity provides in consequence a possibility to benefit from the health care services guaranteed through the public health care system. The possibility to benefit is constrained by the second expression of the right to health, i.e. the right to health care. The nature of this expression of the right to health, the right to health care, does not follow from the same preconditions as the right to the protection of health, and consequently results in different prerogatives. It does not mean, however, that the right to health protection depends on surrounding conditions such as social or economic factors.[212] In fact, the right to the protection of health is absolute and unquestionable. Essentially, the crux of the matter is that the human dignity principle is bound to other fundamental human rights, like the right to life, prohibition of inhuman and degrading treatment, and the right to private life. These concomitant provisions have a crucial meaning to the understanding of the principles that govern the access to health care system. In what follows, as claimed by Hendriks, various aspects of the right to health can be invoked before and applied by Constitutional Courts and other (quasi-) judicial bodies, even though applicants do not always rely on the right to the protec-

212 André Den Exter, Bert Hermans , *op.cit.,* p.263

tion of health itself. [213] The growing legal significance of this right, does not however result in the enhancement of its protection. In reality, the amount of protection granted by courts generally equals and confines itself to a constitutional interpretation of this right, leaving ample discretionary powers to states with respect to their above mentioned core obligation to respect and protect human dignity.

5.1.2 Health as Social Human Right

Typically, the right to health pertains to the category of social human rights, and to a large extent is conditional on how the protection of health on the one hand, and the availability, accessibility and quality of care and cure on the other, have been organised in the national health care system and elaborated in national law. The main characteristics of the social human right is that it requires states to take steps in its progressive realisation, to the full extent of their available resources. As argued previously in Chapter 2, the fact that the constitutional enforceability of such social rights as a right to health care is conditioned upon legislative discretion, is not enough to undermine its justiciability. In short, it was asserted that because of the fact that formal constitutional guarantees must be followed by adequate institutional preconditions, the constitutional review is a tool which allows for the shaping of a given social constitutional right (here: the right to health care). It is not only the matter of checks and balances between state institutions, but also, and to a large extent, it is a matter of a constitutional dialogue, which is to be seen as a careful deliberation of political interests and constitutional premises. It must also be noted, that ever since the introduction of the Limburg Principles[214], the following Vienna Declaration on universality, indivisibility, interdependence and interrelation of all human rights,[215] and the Maastricht Guidelines on Violations of Economic, Social and Cultural Rights,[216] the ideas about the scope and nature of state obligations with respect to social human rights, have shifted towards the recognition of their growing importance. In light of this conceptual change it is perhaps better to attribute to social human rights, including the right to health care, normative, as opposed to programmatic, character in terms of their justiciability and judicial enforcement. By the

213 Aart Hendriks, *op.cit.*, p.392

214 The Limburg Principles on the Implementation of the International Covenant on Economic, Social and Cultural Rights. (1987).

215 Vienna Declaration. (1993).

216 The Maastricht Guidelines on Violations of Economic, Social and Cultural Rights. (1997).

same token, the constitutional right to health care implies a duty to define rules by which the right to protection of health is being put into reality. That is to say, the right to health care entails the setting of a normative structure of reference, which specifies the conditions and scope of health services, and which is functionally oriented towards adequate care and cure.

Even when acknowledging and advocating the shift towards the more substantial normative character of the right to health care, some scholars, like Gevers, recognize the threats to publicly financed health care. Pointing to the everyday reality he admits that there has always been and will always be a discrepancy between what is available on an equal basis for all citizens and their actual needs and demands.[217] According to Gevers, both with regard to the preconditions for health (like a safe and healthy life and working environment), and the availability of adequate care and cure. It does not mean, however, that one should not try to bridge these gaps, nor does it mean that the decisions to be taken with this respect would be free from the everlasting tensions between social solidarity and justice on one hand, and individual freedom and responsibility on the other. It is, therefore, essential to recognise that in spite of the economic and political factors that interfere with underlying principles of solidarity and equality, the right to the protection of health should be a guiding reference in constitutional adjudication on health matters.[218] Given the undeniable interdependence between the individual right to health protection and the social right to health care, it is inevitable that conflicts resulting from attempts to restrict entitlements end up in the legal and constitutional arena. The recognition of the right to health care is therefore conditional, and for this reason it is bounded by limitation clauses, which subject the decisions on the scope and limits of this right to a legislative discretion.

5.1.3 Constitutional Rights to Health (Care)- Comparative Perspective

The right to health protection and health care is recognised in the **Polish Constitution** of 1997 by Article 68, which states in paragraph 1 that:

> *Everyone shall have the right to have his (sic!) health protected.*

and in paragraph 2:

> *Equal access to health care services, financed from public funds, shall be ensured by public authorities to citizens, irrespective of their material situation.*[219]

---

217 Sjef Gevers, *The Right to Health Care*, European Journal of Health Law, No.11 2004, p.30

218 Sjef Gevers, *op.cit.*, p.33

219 Constitution of the Republic of Poland. (1997).

Subsequently, Article 68 para.2 explicitly anticipates limitations to the right to health care stating that the conditions and scope of the provision of health care services shall be established by a statute.[220] It is apparent, that the understanding of the constitutionally guaranteed right to health care, was developed in one of the first rulings of the Constitutional Tribunal with a reference to Article70 para.2 of the Constitution of the People's Republic of Poland. This article provided for a broad formulation for the provisions on the public authorities obligations in securing this right. It has to be noted, that the communist constitution referred to a wider catalogue of state obligations, not only with respect to health care provisions, than the currently applicable Article 68 of the 1997 Constitution.[221] In its subsequent rulings, however, the Constitutional Tribunal acknowledged that although Article70 para.2 displays a lack of precision, what is characteristic for the period of transition, there is a possibility of extracting independent legal content from it; that is, regardless of the systemic shortcomings[222] Article 68 addresses the newly-created, democratic legal-reality and provides for constitutional references that allow the interpretation of this right.

---

220 Article 68 is composed of three other paragraphs that respectively oblige public authorities to: *ensure special health care to children, pregnant women, handicapped people and persons of advanced age* (para.3); *combat epidemic illnesses and prevent the negative health consequences of degradation of the environment* (para.4); *support the development of physical culture, particularly amongst children and young persons* (para.5).

221 Apart from the obligation of "constant improving of safety and hygienic conditions of work which is subject to a broadly developed prevention of illnesses and disease control", Article 70 para.2 of the Constitution of the People's Republic of Poland anticipates a creation of a broad system of social security and, specifically, the development of hospitals, convalescent homes, outpatient clinics and other specific health centres.

222 This explanation was given in the judgement of 22 February 1989 (U 19/88; referred to further in the text) where the reference was made to the Article 70 para.1 of the so called constitutional rules (*przepisy konstytucyjne*) or the upheld constitutional rules (*przepisy konstytucyjne utrzymane w mocy*). Until that time, it was only the Small Constitution (*Mała Konstytucja*) of 17 October 1992 which was in force. The so called Small Constitution was a constitutional act, under a full name "The Constitutional Act of 17 October 1992 on the mutual relations between the legislative and executive institutions of the Republic of Poland and on local self-government". It mostly contained the provisions on the Sejm, the Senate, the President of the Republic of Poland, the Council of Ministers and local self-government. It thus repealed the Constitution of 1952 to this extent of providing for democratic state organs, leaving the remaining provisions in force. For more on the Small Constitution see: Ryszard Chruściak, *The Small Constitution of 1992*, Przegląd Sejmowy, No. 5, 2007.

The constitutional "surrounding", that is the other provision introduced to the constitutional system- such as a new approach to the right to property, a constitutional guarantee of economic freedom (Article 6), a new division of competences between the public and local administration (Article 71 of the Small Constitution), a definition of the civil society (Article 85)- allow to trace a stable and predictable evolution of the constitutional doctrine in the area of constitutional adjudication of the right to health care. The main outcome, of this development is that the general character of the legislator's duties was recognised. The Constitutional Tribunal acknowledged a wide margin of discretion to the Parliament, as to the decision on the scope and form of the future health care legislation. The role of the Tribunal has been defined as limited to interfere only in "drastic situations", once an uncertainty over the scope of the competences and constitutional duties of the legislator has to be clarified. In this context, an interesting definition, which shows the evolution of the constitutional adjudication of the right to health care can be found in the Tribunal's early decision, where this right was interpreted in reference to the right to protection of health, or the right to paid leave (**U.19/88**, decision of 22 February 1989).[223] In this decision the Tribunal made a reference to Article70 para.2 of the Constitution of the People's Republic of Poland, which provided that the citizens of the People's Republic of Poland have a right to the protection of health, which "is subject to constant improving of safety and hygienic conditions of work and which is subject to a broadly developed prevention of illnesses and disease control."

When analyzing former constitutional judgements, it is apparent that the Constitutional Tribunal denied the conception of the subjective right with respect to the right of health care. Still in reference to the 1952 Constitution, the Tribunal affirmed in its ruling **K 7/90** of 22 August 1990 that the legislator enjoys the discretion to define the nature and scope of the constitutionally enshrined right to health care.[224] The Tribunal confirmed this point of view in a number of cases, where it considered the provisions providing citizens with a guarantee of the right to health care in case of sickness, old age, and other situations.[225] At the same time, the Tribunal accepted the subsequent obligation of

223 Published in Z.U. 1989//11; OTK1986-1995/t2/1989/11.

224 Pension provision for employees and their families, K 7/90, (The Polish Constitutional Tribunal 22 August 1990).

225 E.g. Pension provision for Radio and Television employees and their families, K 1/88, (The Polish Constitutional Tribunal 30 November 1988). Pension provision for employees and their families- Solidarity of Work Veterans, K 6/91, (The Polish Constitutional Tribunal 23March 1992). Disability and old-age pensions, K 14/91, (The Polish Constitutional Tribunal 11 March 1992);Employment and pensions provision, K 14/92, (The Polish Constitutional Tribunal 19 October 1993).

the state to materialise such a guarantee. However, it defined this obligation as limited to the provision of a "minimum level of services". Moreover, it underlined that by no means there had been a place for individual entitlements,[226] but, as the Tribunal noticed, the legislator was given a far-reaching discretionary power to shape the necessary regulation provided that it complied with other constitutional norms and principles. Legislative discretion to regulate the conditions and scope of the constitutional social rights is not, however, an absolute prerogative. According to the constitutional doctrine, the legislator is bound by its constitutional duties to provide for specific laws in adequate areas, and thus, principles such as the principle of legal certainty, the principle of public trust, or the principle of confidence in laws oblige the legislator to introduce laws that are complete, precise and unequivocal. These principles were invoked in the Polish Constitutional Tribunal ruling on the national health care security system (**P 7/03** of 28 February 2005). Here the Court said that the right to health care stipulated in Article 68 para.2 of the Polish Constitution, should not be regarded as simple authorisation of the legislator to define the conditions and scope of the health care provisions. The Tribunal explicitly stated that the legislator has a duty to provide for such conditions and the scope of health provisions that would assure "*confidence of the beneficiaries, stability of legal rules, and would allow an individual for a long-term planning to safeguard their needs beyond the public system.*" *Ergo*, by guaranteeing the stability of legal rules, the state is obliged to create a system within which the "*individual is able to take up his/her responsibility to take care of him/herself.*" A duty to legislate should not be subjected to the determination of a simple framework that allows the fulfilment of the right or its *essentialia negotii.* The Polish Tribunal underlined that it is not only the privilege of the legislator to "translate" the constitutional provisions into ordinary legislation. It is also their duty to legislate in accordance with such principles (such as principle of a sufficient determination of law - *dostatecznej określoności prawa*). This means that once the Constitution imposes the duty to legislate, the legal act needs to provide for "complete, precise and unequivocal provisions". What is more, the Tribunal affirmed that the legislator takes on a responsibility for "coherence, clarity and completeness" of legal solutions, which are illustrated in the judgement of 23 January 2003 (**Ref. No. K 14/03**) on public health security in the National Health Fund. In this ruling the Tribunal was reminded that the Constitution does not define the scope of health care services available to all citizens, by referring this competence to the ordinary legis-

226 At the same time the Tribunal reminded a widely accepted rule in the Polish constitutional adjudication doctrine, saying that the legal basis for individual entitlements can only be derived from concrete constitutional norms achieved by means of legislation.

lation. This reference is due to the so called "limitation clause", which subjects the conditions and scope of the particular regulation to the act of the ordinary legislation.

The **Czech Charter on Fundamental Rights and Basic Freedoms** guarantees the right to the protection of health and the right to health care in Article 31. The article reads as follows:

> *Everyone has the right to the protection of his (sic!) health. Citizens shall have the right, on the basis of public insurance, to free medical care and to medical aids under conditions provided for by law.*[227]

Under the current constitutional doctrine, this article stipulates that everybody has a right to health care. Every citizen, who financially contributes to the public health care system, has a right to free public medical services, which are defined in the ordinary act. This means, that the legislator is given the right to set up the scope and form of the public health care system and services comprised therein. The provision on the legislator's discretion is re-confirmed by a separate provision, provided for in Article 41 para.1 of the Charter. This article enumerates all the constitutional rights that are subordinated to the conditions provided for in the ordinary legislation act. Contrary to the Polish solution, where the limitation clause relating to the right to health care, is mentioned only in the article relating to health care, the Czech constitutional legislator decided to repeat the limitation clause in a separate article. Article 81 of the Polish Constitution provides for a limiting clause to other, explicitly enumerated, constitutional rights. The right to health care, however, is not mentioned there. The Czech solution, does not seem to impose a tighter constraint on the Constitutional Court, once it adjudicates in health care matters. According to the Czech constitutional jurisprudence, the constitutionally guaranteed right to health care is binding upon the legislator, since the Charter imposes a valid commitment on the legislator, which must be performed, and which is understood as a constitutional duty of the legislator. In 1996 a case on the introduction of patients' out-of-pocket payments by a ministerial resolution (Ordinance) was brought before the Constitutional Court.[228] The case, indeed, concerned a political controversy around the phrase "*under conditions provided for by law*" stipulated in Article 31 of the Charter. According to Article 41 para.1, the right as provided for by Article 31 of the Charter may only be claimed "*within the confines of the laws implementing these provisions*". This

227 Constitutional Act no. 2/1993 Coll., Charter of Fundamental Rights and Basic Freedoms, as subsequently amended. (1993).

228 Patients' out-of-pocket payments, Pl. ÚS 35/95, (The Constitutional Court of the Czech Republic 10 July 1996).

means, that the limitations of these specified constitutional rights require an explicit statutory basis. The ministerial Ordinance was considered insufficient in this case, and the Court ruled that the procedure used for introducing patients' co-payments for basic health care services violated the constitutional right to health care.

The Czech Constitutional Court dealt with defining the right to health care with regard to the public finance reform that came into effect in January 2007. In view of the complexity of the reform, the Court has decided to divide the case brought by the opposition party into three parts. The Court distinguished the question on procedural and taxation matters (part one, **Pl. ÚS 24/07** of 31 January 2008), sickness-leave benefits (part two, **Pl. ÚS 2/08** of 23 April 2008), and the so called "doctor fees". Although the Court dealt with the procedure of the implementation of the complex reform package, especially by referring to previous year's case on the so called *přílepky* (**Pl. ÚS 77/06** of 15 February 2007), it came back to the issue of the comprehensibility and internal consistency of the law when dealing with the specific issue of short-term sickness-leave benefits. Interestingly, the Court said that notwithstanding its consent on the constitutionality of the procedure in which the law was enacted, it remains concerned about weak legal consistency of the already enacted laws. In this ruling the Court dealt with the problem that the provisions remain heavily unspecified (*neurčitost*). Similar observations on the incompliance with the principle of legal certainty and foresight of the law were evoked in the Court's earlier judgements, namely in the judgement on Pension Insurance (**II.ÚS 405/22** of 3 June 2004). This case concerned differentiation between citizens of the Czech Republic in the "employment abroad" context of Czech citizens employed in Slovakia during the period of the Czechoslovak state. The case of Basic Principles (**Pl.ÚS 2/02** of 9 March 2004), however, unrelated to social and economic matters, provides a broad interpretation of the principle of the law-based state in connection with such principles as the principle of legal certainty, the principle of trust in law, the foresight of the law, its comprehensibility and internal consistency. In this case the Court refers to the Strasbourg ruling on *Hentrich v. France* in evoking the principle of lawfulness. The Czech Court thus followed ECtHR's definition of the lawfulness, saying that it presupposes a sufficiently accessible, precise and foreseeable domestic legal norm.

The right to health protection and health care in the **Constitution of the Slovak Republic** is enshrined in Article 40. Its formulation is very similar to the one of the Polish Constitution and Czech Charter, in a way that it provides a right to health care to everybody, and that it subjects the scope of the public health care system to the legislator's discretion.

> *Everyone shall have the right to protection of his or her health. The citizens shall have the right to free health care and medical equipment for disabilities on the basis of medical insurance under the terms to be laid down by law.*[229]

Apart from that, the Slovak Constitution provides for a separate, more detailed and directed right to health care for women, minors and disabled persons with extensive health protection at work. Interestingly enough, the Slovak constitutional doctrine developed in the field of the constitutional right to health care, stipulates that the state's duty to guarantee to an individual a necessary health care service is not absolute.[230] It depends on the will of an ill person to receive medical assistance provided by the state. Moreover, only the Slovak official English translation of the constitutional provision on health care, explicitly stipulates equal access to the health care (system) regardless of sex. This remark seems to hold only for the Constitutions in their English translation, since the inequality in access to health services based on sex, has never been an issue in any of the constitutional jurisprudence of the three countries.

A similar solution to the limitation clause used in the Slovak Constitution in reference to the right to health care, was accepted by the Polish constitutional legislator. The discretion of the ordinary legislator is laid down only in Article 40. However, contrary to the Polish and Czech determination of legislative discretion assigned to the determination of the conditions, and the scope of the health care services, the Slovak provision was extended to a stipulation which also ensures medical equipment for the disabled. This is similar to the Czech constitutional solution. The right to health protection and health care is formulated in one, uniform article. It may suggest that the distinction between the two expressions of the right to health, in general, will be difficult to follow. The textual interpretation of this article suggests, on the other hand, a strong link between these two aspects of the right to health.

---

229 Vienna Declaration.

230 Ján Drgonec, *Základné práva a slobody podľa Ústavy Slovenskej republiky,* MANZ, 1999, p.202.

5.2 Right to Social Security According to Constitutional Jurisprudence- Comparative Perspective

Under the current **Polish Constitution**, the right to social security is guaranteed in Article 67 and since it is not subject to general limiting clause, it is considered as a directly justiciable constitutional right. The article states explicitly that citizens are entitled to the right to social security in case of incapacity for work, sickness and disability, as well as in the case of retirement. Section 2 of this Article stipulates that social security benefits are also granted to citizens in case of unemployment. Both, section 1 and 2 are subject to concrete limitation clauses, which establish that the form and scope of the right to social security in these particular cases shall be established by statute. It was not clear, especially as it stems from the early jurisprudence of the Constitutional Tribunal, whether the right to social security may be used as a basis for individual claims. In fact, the reason for this was the statute of the upheld constitutional rules and consequential constitutional framework in which the Tribunal could have interpreted the right to social security.

Until 1997, the right to social security was specified in Article 70 of the 1952 Constitution (with further amendments) and later of the upheld constitutional rules (u.c.r.). Article 70.1 u.c.r. provided for both the right to the protection of health and to social security to citizens of the Peoples' Republic of Poland. In section 2 sentence 1 of this article, it has been further determined that the realisation of the right to social security is attained by the development of social security benefits in case of sickness, old age, and inability to work, as well as by expansion of different forms of social assistance.[231] This approach guarantees social security benefits, and at the same time it maintains an obligation to develop a social security system. Above all, these provisions created challenges in the period of the financial reforms of the 1990s which by aiming at transformation to free market economy envisaged restrictions to public expenditure and cuts of the generous benefits. On the one hand in its jurisprudence the Tribunal referred to provisions resulting from Art. 70 as general guarantees for old-age and disability pensions, and said that they necessitate an obligation of the state to maintain at least the minimum of these benefits on an appropriate level. The Tribunal claimed at the same time that the provisions of this article do not create legal claims for individuals and it recognised the far-reaching discre-

231 Own translation of provisions of Article 70 of the Constitution of the People's Republic of Poland, proclaimed on 22 July 1952, as amended. Copy with the author.

tion of the legislator in deciding on the scope of these benefits.[232] Still, the Tribunal underlined that the legislative discretion is bound by an obligation to respect other constitutional principles and norms.

In defining the content of Art.70 in the **K 1/88** judgement, the Tribunal paid attention to the already mentioned three constituent elements of the right to social security: 1) benefits of citizens in case of sickness and inability to work, 2) establishment of the social security system, and 3) obligation of the State to develop the right to social security governed by the principle of *progressive development*.[233] At the same time, the Tribunal confirmed that the Constitution recognises the power of legislator to decide upon the types of benefits available within the social security system, the conditions of acquirement and termination of the benefits, the rates of various types of benefits, the procedures of granting benefits, etc.[234] With regard to types, rates and management of the social benefits, in the early 1990s, the legislator had to decide on the point of the departure for the management of the social security system. Numerous questions of particular importance over whether to maintain the rates and types of the benefits already granted, how to deal with the exigencies of economic reforms such as budget cuts, became more and more pressing in the transforming economy. In its early jurisprudence therefore, the Court was often faced with fundamental questions concerning the nature of the right to social security and the subsequent legal consequences of its constitutional nature. Interpretation of the progressive development principle shows how the Court embarked upon its jurisprudence but also shows how the Court has changed its position in this respect over the course of time.

At the beginning the Court gave an indication which assumed that the obligation aiming at progressive development of social security system means a prohibition of "worsening of conditions [...] that result from statutory law binding at the time of enactment of new statutes".[235] The criterion of time accepted as a starting

232 Case Pension provision for RTV employees and their families [1988] K 1/88, Case Pension provision for employees and their families [1990] K 7/90; also confirmed in SK 27/02, K 5/99 and SK 30/03

233 Case Pension provision for RTV employees and their families [1988] K 1/88, p.8

234 K 7/90

235 K 1/88; also U 7/87 The departure point to maintenance of the current situation, was however, expressly defined and specified in the same judgment. It was the day of introduction of the 1952 Constitution. It meant that the reference was made to then binding statutory regulations as well as ILO Conventions to which the People's Republic was party of. See in: K 1/88

point was the enactment of the Constitution of 1952,[236] however, the Court repeatedly underlined the obligation to develop the system in *harmony with the economic situation* in the country.[237] At the same time, however, the Court acknowledged the limits of the possible reference to the economic situation by the legislator, by establishing what later was called "a test for the *optimality of statute*". The optimality test was established as a subordinate condition to the repeatedly stated affirmation of the Tribunal so that it does not assess usefulness or purposefulness of a given legal solution, but it leaves such decisions to the discretion of the legislator. The test was based on the assumption that the established legal provisions were the only possible ones and were based on a precondition of optimality with the view of the aims of the law under review. By and large, the test came as a result of judgments over statutes concerning the reform of wages and questions concerning indexation of wages, in defence of which the legislator voiced economic preconditions in the form of the "economic state of necessity".[238] The Tribunal said, however, that although it has previously recognised that the "*drastic breakdown of the budgetary balance* may constitute a basis for limitation, or even temporary abolishment of the indexation of wages",[239] it refuses to admit that the existence of the state of economic necessity can be introduced by statutory provisions. The Tribunal said that such an extraordinary means could only be introduced if they were expressed in the Constitution. Instead, the argument on the drastic breakdown of the budgetary balance was further developed by the Tribunal. It was conditioned upon two other reservations. The Tribunal said that the legislator needs to demonstrate that it made sure that the distribution of budgetary means is appropriate [240] and that it exhausted all the possible means to ascertain the ways to increase budgetary revenue.[241]

It is unquestionable that although the Tribunal accepted arguments referring to the economic situation of the state, it reserved the power to assess regulations according to the criteria of the equality of the financial burden and the rational choice of the legislator, leaving the Tribunal with a lot of influence.[242] Therefore

---

236 Statement confirmed in a number of judgements: K 7/90, K 14/91, K 10/92. The Tribunal said that obligation of the State to develop the system of social insurance is "conditional upon economic development of the State" (K 14/92) and that this obligation may be executed if "the economic situation allows for it" (K 7/90).

237 See for example judgement K 10/92.

238 See for example: K 4/91

239 See in: K 15/91

240 In Polish: *prawidłowość rozdziału środków budżetowych,* K 15/91

241 See: K 18/92

242 In the *acquis constituionelle* in reference to these matters, it seems to be clear that the Tribunal does not intend to restrain its powers.

from the very beginning, the Tribunal on the one hand recognised legislative discretion on the materialisation of the rights to social security, while at the same time it also highlighted the limits that constrained the legislator in the performance of the constitutional duties. As it was referred to above, one of the constraints was recognised in the obligation of the legislator to develop the system of social security benefits. The other limitation, also derived from Art. 70 and concerned the respect of the essence of the right to social security.[243] As in other circumstances the Tribunal took from the German constitutional tradition in referring to the dual character of every constitutional right and freedom and the resultant distinction of the essence (that remains beyond the competences of the legislator) and the entourage (that the legislator is able to influence). The essence of the various forms of the right to social security was defined by the Court in numerous judgements over the years.[244] The essence of the right to social benefit in the case of retirement for example, sets limits on the time-interval within the framework with which the legislator has a right to define the age of retirement (in practice this statement follows a simple logic: the older the insured citizen is, the longer the period of his/her professional activity, and consequently the longer the period of his/her insurance). Besides, identity of this right is ensured through the assurance of the minimum standard of living conditions so that the basic needs of life are guaranteed.[245] Essentially, there are at least three basic elements to which the Tribunal often refers to as to elements that constitute the essence of the right to social security. These are: 1) statutory modifications cannot deprive citizens from the right to social security; 2) statutory modifications cannot violate minimum standards of living; 3) system of social security is understood as a "system of obligatory benefits stemming from the fact of work (…)". [246]

As it can be observed, the Tribunal recognized the right given to the legislator to define the details of particular constitutional rights. Nevertheless, the Tribunal said that still, the substance and limits of rights are directly shaped by constitutional norms. An example of this approach can be found in the judgment

243 K 7/90, K 14/92

244 Attempts to define the essence of the various forms of the right to social security did not come until the 1997 Constitution mainly because until that time the Tribunal chose to refer to constitutional principles as an indirect source of interpretation of the right, rather than directly to Art.70 u.c.r.

245 See for example judgements: K 5/99, SK 27/02, SK 30/03.

246 Leszek Garlicki, *Prawa socjalne w orzecznictwie Trybunału Konstytucyjnego*, Przegląd Sejmowy, 1995, p.62-63

of 20 December 1999 on the valorisation of old-age and disability pensions.[247] The Polish Tribunal said that "it is beyond the Tribunal's competence to judge whether the legislator have found the most correct and most proper settlement of the legislated issue". In other words, the Tribunal recognizes the legislator's discretion to decide upon the best solution. The second solution to the "limitation clause" presupposes that the definition of the content and substance of the particular rights are left to legislative discretion. Notwithstanding the wide-reaching freedom of the legislator, according to the current constitutional doctrine, rights that are subject to the limitation clause of the second type have the full normative power of constitutional provisions, and may be subject to constitutional review.[248]

The right to social security (*sociální zabezpečení*) in the **Czech Charter** is formulated in three paragraphs of Article 30, two of which address the right itself, while the third provides for a concrete limiting clause. The right to social security is understood partly as a citizens' right (*právo občanské*), and partly as a human right (*právo lidské*). It says that the right to adequate material security in old age and during periods of work incapacity, as well as in the case of the loss of their provider[249] is guaranteed to the citizens (paragraph 1), while the right to assistance to the extent to which it is necessary to ensure basic living standards is referred to as the right of "everyone" (paragraph 2). The applicability of the right stemming from paragraph 1 defined by actual executing legislation relates to "residents with permanent residence permit on the territory of the Czech Republic" and is not granted on the basis of citizenship.[250] The controversy over the applicability of the right to social security benefits based on the citizenship came up with numerous individual complaints concerning the so-

247 See: K 4/99

248 In its famous judgment of 4 April 2001 K 11/00 known as the "eviction to nowhere case" (*eksmisja na bruk*), the Polish Tribunal said that although Art. 71 of the Constitution cannot be a direct basis for the citizen's claims, it recognizes a view expressed in the constitutional doctrine that the infringement of the constitutional provision determining the aims of activities carried out by the public authorities takes also place when "the legislator wrongly interprets the provision of the Constitution (…), by adopting a law prescribing means that could not lead to achieving that goal…" (J. Trzciński, Commentary on Article 79 paragraph 1 of the Constitution of the Republic of Poland, *Konstytucja Rzeczypospolitej Polskiej. Komentarz*, Vol. I, Warszawa 1999).

249 In this case, the exceptional circumstance covers widows and orphans. The doctrine also allows an interpretation stating that the situation concerns widowers, although it is not so evident as in the case of widowed women. See: V. Pavlíček., *Ústava a ústavní řád České republiky…*, p.248.

250 V. Pavlíček., *Ibid.*

called Czechoslovak pensions,[251] the effect of the one of the separation-related treaties between the Czech Republic and Slovakia dealing with social security and pension benefit issues. The basic rule adopted therein established that a pension should be paid by the state of the registered seat of a legal entity for which an individual had worked.[252] Growing disparity between economic conditions in Slovakia with comparison to the situation in the Czech Republic resulted in a situation where pensions paid to people who worked on the territory of the Czech Republic became considerably higher than those who worked in Slovakia. The position of the Czech nationals, who after retirement mostly lived in the Czech Republic, but had worked for Czech companies registered in the territory of Slovakia before 1993 worsened significantly. According to the law, they were entitled to considerably lower Slovak pensions. In numerous cases brought through constitutional complaints, the Czech Constitutional Court decided that the pension claims of these people should be calculated with reference to their Czech citizenship.[253] One of the important aspects that was brought up in the complaints was that the Czech citizens have found themselves in the situation in which, according to the law, they were considered to be working abroad. This fact undoubtedly had a negative impact on their pension entitlements within the Czech pension insurance system. The Court rejected this argument by saying

---

251 II. ÚS 405/02 of 3 June 2003; III. ÚS 252/04 of 25 January 2005; IV. ÚS 158/04 of 4 April 2005.

252 See: Art. 20 of the *Smlouva mezi Českou republikou a Slovenskou republikou o sociálním zabezpečení* [Treaty on Social Security between the Czech Republic and the Slovak Republic], Act no. 228/1993 Coll. This article also provided that the regulation concerns those individuals who were self-employed and worked on a given state's territory.

253 There is considerable controversy between the Czech Constitutional and Supreme Administrative Courts on this issue. In its two judgements, 3 Ads 2/2003-60 of 19 February 2004 and 6 Ads 62/2003-31 of 23 February 2005, the Supreme Administrative Court claimed that entitlements under social security laws cannot be based on citizenship, but rather on the territory of an individual's actual place of work. In this respect, the Supreme Administrative Court referred to Community legislation which bounds the eligibility to social benefits with the notion of residence, and not the one of citizenship. This fact is commented upon by the Czech scholars as a breach of Community law by the Czech Constitutional Court, to the extent to which it establishes discrimination based on nationality. Nevertheless, in defence of the Constitutional Court's position it is claimed that on the one hand the facts and the legal regime concerns an extraordinary situation of the dissolution of the state and the group of people concerned is a closed one. See: Michał Bobek, *A new legal order, or a non-existent one? Some (early) experiences in the application of the EU law in Central Europe*, Croatian Yearbook of European Law and Policy, Vol.2, 2006, pp.265-298, p. 275-276; J. Zemánek, *The Emerging Czech Constitutional Doctrine of European Law,* EuConst, No. 3, 2007, pp. 418-435, p. 421.

that "the differentiation between citizens of the Czech Republic, which is based on a fiction that employment in the Slovak Republic of the joint Czechoslovak state is 'employment abroad', to be discriminatory as it is not supported by 'objective' and 'reasonable' grounds.[254] The court held that with respect to the principle of equality and equal access to social security, all Czech citizens should be entitled to the same pensions, irrespective of the fact whether they worked on Czech or Slovak territory prior to the split of the Czechoslovak Federation.

Yet in another case that referred to the 1995 Act on Pension Security, the Court dealt with the issue of awarding privileged additional benefits to certain categories of disabled workers, namely to former miners. In the case on *Equality in Social Legislation,* **Pl. ÚS 15/02** of 21 January 2003, the Court held that the preferential treatment of former miners was based upon objective and reasonable criteria, such as physically and mentally demanding work under harsh conditions. In this respect, the Court took a stand that not every equal treatment of persons has to be considered as a breach of the principle of equality.

5.3 Right to Education

From among social constitutional rights, the right to education draws attention primarily because of its special cross-sectoral character.[255] It is often deemed that the right to education not only influences a number of spheres of our lives, but also is dependant on the performance of rights protection from other sectors. What does the right to education entail?

In a wider perspective, the right to education is perceived as a protective measure against economic exploitation. Not only children are subject to such

254 See: judgement II. ÚS 405/02 of 3 June 2003. Also there, when addressing the "objective and reasonable grounds", the Court referred to provisions of the Czech National Council's Constitutional Act no. 4/1993 Coll., on Measures Connected with the Dissolution of the Czech and Slovak Federal Republic, which provided for the transposition of the CSFR legal order in the Czech law. Thus, the Czech Republic accepted the principle of continuity of the legal order at the constitutional level. Moreover the joint Czechoslovak state had a uniform pension insurance system, and so in terms of the law at the time, it was legally irrelevant in which part of Czechoslovakia the citizen was employed. Nor was it significant where his/her employer had a seat. Therefore, the period of employment with an employer whose registered address was in the Slovak part of Czechoslovakia cannot be seen as "employment abroad".

255 Ida. E Koch, *The Right to Education as a Means and an End in itself- the Indivisibility, Interdependence and Interrelation of human rights*, The Danish Institute for Human Rights 2001.

danger, but it is a widely observed fact that educated individuals who are able to take care of themselves, for example, in employment situations are less vulnerable in terms of economic malpractice. An educated individual would have a chance to protect him/herself from abuses of various kind, or would be able to identify them and prevent them. The protective measure against economic exploitation by employers is for example, expressed by a fixed age for admission to employment. Linked to the right of education is also the right to work in the sense that it increases the possibilities of obtaining a well-paid job.[256] Again, an educated individual is capable of taking care of him/herself. This has consequences for the function and design of social security and old-age security systems. Not only is education becoming an important determinant of living standards, as more and more jobs require concrete skills and knowledge. It is now clear that some groups, i.e. illiterate, will be more exposed to exclusion from the labour market, hence they have fewer possibilities to lift themselves out of poverty. According to the UN Special Rapporteur on education, primary schooling will only function as key to poverty reduction to the extent to which it is actually provided free of charge.[257] Investment in education is one of the best investments a state can make, and it is an essential key to long-term economic and social development.[258]

The important link between education and health is also made evident. Recently, the focus on the importance of information about how to protect oneself against various diseases, and infections, how to live a healthy and balanced life seems to be a predominant concern to states and sub-national organisations, such as the European Union. This aspect becomes even more relevant when confronted with the phenomena of aging societies. The knowledge of basic and more elaborate health protection intends to shift the responsibility from the state to individuals to arrange for adequate measures of health protection, but at the same time concentrates the responsibility on the state to inform its citizens on various developments in medicine, so that the society mainly has access to knowledge and information. Having regard to education aspect, it is possible that the meaning of the right to health would gain a new perspective. Yet, the impact on the right to education within the sphere of civil and political rights is positive. This mainly relates to the right to participate as education is a precondi-

---

256 The interdependence of social and economic rights proven by research of the Massachusetts Institute of Technology (MIT) http://www.povertyactionlab.org/research/Education%20MDGs.pdf

257 Cf. The Annual Report of 11 January 2001 of Special Rapporteur on the right to education; see: Ida. E Koch, *ibid*, fn 9, p.3

258 Ida. E Koch, *op.cit.*, p.3

tion of the right to vote for political representation, and it is necessary for seeking and receiving information, but also for the freedom of expression, assembly and association. A holistic vision of civil and political rights and social and economic rights can certainly be noticed through the lenses of the realisation of the right to education. Moreover, this argument is confirmed by the fact that the reference to equality and non-discrimination principles are fundamental to the right to education, and thus, for example disparities in education have consequences far beyond education itself. In this way, discrimination leads to unequal wages, unequal career possibilities, unequal political representation, etc. and this is essential to living standards, opportunities and options in life. Therefore, providing education is one of the best methods to promote equality opportunity.[259] Additionally, "education has a positive key-function in the sense that it unlocks the doors to other rights. As important to remember is, however, that denial of the right to education amounts to a denial of a number of other human rights, social and civil. The right to education is a *conditio sine qua non*".[260]

Overall, the right to education may be considered as an "empowerment" right, understood as a right which enables a person to benefit from other rights because it is linked to other rights. Such a departure point focusing on an individual, by acknowledging that an educated citizen is able to make use of other rights granted to him/her by the constitution, because of the ability to give meaning to the rest of these rights.[261]

5.3.1 Constitutional Right to Education- Comparative Perspective

The Constitutional right to education was formulated for the first time in the French Constitution of 1791. Most commonly, constitutional right to education is considered as a subjective right.[262] It is often linked to the provision of free system of public schooling.[263]

---

259 Manfred Nowak, *The Right to Education*, in: Asbjørn Eide et al. (ed*.), Economic, Social and Cultural Rights – A Textbook*, Martinus Nijhoff Publ., The Hague 1995, p.198.

260 Ida. E Koch, *op.cit.*, p.4

261 Fons Coomans, *In Search of the Core Content of the Right to Education*, in: Audrey Chapman, Sage Russell (eds.), *Core Obligations: Building a Framework for Economic and Cultural Rights*, Insertia, Antwerp, Oxford, New York, 2002, p.219-220.

262 Art.24.3 of Belgian Constitution of 1831; art.42.3 of the Irish Constitution of 1937; art.34.1 of the Italian Constitution of 1957; para. 76 of the Danish Constitution of 1953; art.21 of the Swedish Act on the Government of 1974; art.16.4 of the Greek Constitution of 1957; art.74.1 of the Portuguese Constitution of 1976; art. 27.1 of the Spanish Constitution of 1978; para.16 of the Finish Constitution of 1999; art.19 of the Swiss constitution of 1999); Constitution of Bulgaria of 1991, Constitution of Romania of

Among other most popular formulations of the right to education, one may find a separate guarantee to establish private schools, and guarantees of autonomy for the schools at the university level. Although the formulations refer to similar goals, they are nevertheless different in terms of literal precision and thus, are not exactly the same.

For example, the right to education in the Latvian Constitution is formulated as follows:

> *"Freedom of education shall be guaranteed. Primary education is compulsory and shall be financed from public funds. The state shall create the opportunities for citizens to obtain a proper education."*[264]

First of all this expression does not refer to the right to education but provides for freedom of education. Moreover it does not give a clear indication as to who are the addressees of the freedom of education.[265] Nor is it clear who should

---

1991, the Charter of Fundamental Rights and Basic Freedoms of the Czech Republic, Constitution of Estonia of 1992, Constitution of Lithuania of 1992, Constitution of Slovakia of 1992, Russian Constitution of 1993, Constitution of Ukraine of 1996, Constitution of Albania of 1998, Constitution of Latvia as amended in 1998, Constitution of Poland of 1997, Slovenia. See in: Kazimierz Działocha, Paweł Sarnecki, Wojciech Sokolewicz, *Konstytucja Rzeczypospolitej Polskiej: Komentarz III*, Leszek Garlicki (ed.), Wydawnictwo Sejmowe, Warszawa, 2003.

263 Art.24.2 of the Belgian Constitution; para.12 of the Introduction to the French Constitution of 1946; art.34.2 of the Italian Constitution; para.76 of the Danish Constitution; art.16.4 of the Greek Constitution. Limited to primary schools in: the Irish Constitution-art.42.3; Portuguese Constitution-art.74.2; Swedish Act on the Government-art.21; Spanish Constitution-art.27.4; the Finish Constitution-para.16.1; Swiss Constitution-art.19; Bulgarian Constitution- art.53.3; Constitution of Romania-art.34.2; Czech Charter- art.33.2; Constitution of Estonia- para.37.1; Lithuanian Constitution- art.41.2; Slovak Constitution- art.42.1; Russian Constitution- art.43.2-3; Ukrainian Constitution-art.3.3-4; Albanian Constitution- art.57.5; Latvian Constitution- art.112. Some constitutions limit the right to free public education to primary schools only, ex: para. 70F.2 of the Hungarian Constitution of 1949; art.65.1 of the Croatian Constitution of 1990; art.44.3 of Macedonian Constitution of 1991; art.57.3 of the Slovenian Constitution of 1991. See in: Kazimierz Działocha, Paweł Sarnecki, Wojciech Sokolewicz, *op.cit.*

264 Art.112 of the Constitution of the Republic of Latvia. Adopted by the Constitutional Assembly of the Republic of Latvia on 15 February 1922.

265 The right to education is verbalised in Article 52 and is given to physically or mentally handicapped children and other severely disabled persons. More interestingly, Article 64 of the Slovene Constitution gives the right to education and bi-lingual schooling to members of the Italian and Hungarian national communities in Slovenia. No other minorities are given such a right. Furthermore, this right is defined in much more detail by refereeing the establishment of bilingual schools to ordinary law and indicating sate's responsibilities towards

provide for the education. It is certainly arguable that the state should provide for it, but the constitution does not clearly oblige it to do so. The state is made responsible for creating opportunities for citizens to obtain a proper education, but not held accountable for the failure to provide education. To the contrary, the Estonian Constitution by Article 37 confers greater responsibility on the government by stating in the third sentence that:

> *"(i)n order to make education accessible, the State and local governments shall maintain the requisite number of institutions",*

and further:

> *"(t)he provision of education shall be supervised by the State."*

This provision is preceded by a statement, saying that:

> *"(e)veryone has the right to education. Education is compulsory for school-age children to the extent specified by law, and shall be free of charge in State and local government general education schools".*

This article therefore identifies the state as responsible for the supervision of education in the country and maintenance of the requisite number of educational institutions. According to Article 37 everyone has the right to education, which is already a clearer definition of the addresses of the right, further strengthened by the provision saying that compulsory education for school-age children shall be free of charge in state and local government general education schools. The only limitation is that the formulation "to the extent specified by law", but it refers to the definition of the school-age. In sum, the overall expression of the duty of the state to provide for schools and supervise education does not create doubt whether it is the state or any other entity which is obliged to provide the education.

5.3.2 The Right to Education According to Constitutional Jurisprudence- Comparative Perspective

The analysis of the right to education, as stipulated in the **Polish Constitution** of 1997 provides for a wide normative content. Article 70, not only establishes the right to education as such but endows it with the main characteristics, like obli-

---

realisation of this right, i.e. "(…) *The State shall provide material and moral support for the exercise of these rights.*" To the contrary again the Estonian Constitution takes entirely distinct standpoint. In its fourth paragraph Article 37 says that: "*Everyone has the right to receive instruction in Estonian*", and further restricts education in minority languages to specialised educational institutions by stating that: "*The language of instruction in national minority educational institutions shall be chosen by the educational institutions*".

gatory education until the age of 18 (sentences 1 and 2 of Art.70 para.1), or universal and equal access to education (sentence 1, Art.70 para.4). It also provides for the freedom to choose and establish schools (sentence 1 and 2 of Art.70 para.3), as well as defining characteristics of the system of education (paragraphs 2, 3 and 5). In general, the right to education is defined by the Polish constitutional doctrine as a separate, subjective right, which is seen, at the same time, as a premise to the realisation of other individual rights and freedoms. Its content provides for the possibility of acquiring knowledge, of a regular and integral instruction given in organised forms, which leads to receiving recognised proofs of education that ensure either a possibility to continue the education or to take up employment.[266] Article 70 para.1 introduces an obligatory education. This is an exceptional formulation as compared to the rest of socio-economic rights that are expressed as "ability rights", and therefore as such these rights provide the way and the extent to which their addresses deem to make or not to make use of them. Still, the right to education in the Polish Constitution was considered so important, that it was formulated as a universal obligation. Although widely formulated, the right to education is not an absolute one. Its concrete formulation is subject to the legislator's competences.

Further, with respect to the right to education as laid down in the Polish Constitution of 1997, two aspects should be distinguished. On the one hand, realisation of the right to education requires an effort on the part of the state to make education available and accessible. It therefore requires positive state obligation, as the state is compelled to organise and supervise the system of education. Article 70 formulates more specific guarantees that assume the concrete obligations of the state, such as specific constitutional principles of the system of education: first, the principle of three level education (primary, secondary and universities/higher schools) stemming form Art.70 para.3, sentence 2; second, the guarantee of the functioning of public and non-public education stemming from Article 70 para.3 sentence 1 and sentence 2; and third, the principle of autonomy of the institutions of higher education as formulated in Art.70 para.5. Free public education, as laid down in Art. 70 para.2, subjects the function of public schools to public means, and confirms the freedom to establish non-public schools which may define tuition and other fees, implying that they can make a profit, what consequently is an element of the freedom of economic activity as stipulated in Article 22 of the Constitution. On the other hand, there is the freedom aspect of the right to education, that is the freedom of individuals to choose either to receive education from public or non-public

266 J. Mikosz, *Prawo do nauki*, in: *Prawa człowieka. Model prawny*, Ossolineum 1991, p.1009-1010.

schools, or to establish their own education entities. The right to education in this respect also refers to the addressees who are either all individuals until the age of 18, or their parents who have the right to ensure their children's education, also moral and religious according to their own beliefs. This aspect of the right of education requires the state to follow a policy of non-interference in private matters, and implies negative state obligations. It also implies claims from the individuals to whom this right applies. The doctrine is however, divided over whether the right to education can be considered as a classic social right which assumes that individuals can make use of the possibilities available in order to materialize this right, or whether the scope of the right to education also implies a prohibition that the state undertakes actions that would possibly menace individuals' freedom of choice.[267]

The right to education in the **Czech Charter** is granted to everybody and is linked to the obligation of school attendance (Art.33 para.1). The age until which the school attendance is obligatory is subjected to statutory regulation. Further, the right to education is given three concrete aspects. First, is the aspect of a free education (Art. 33 para.2), second the freedom to establish and to teach in schools other than public schools (Art. 33 para.3), and third the eligibility for financial assistance for students from public funds (Art. 33 para.4). The doctrine notices the particularity of the right to education which imposes compulsory full-time education. The Charter describes obligatory education to all individuals and subjects its further details, together with setting of the age limit, to statutory regulation. Provided that the notion of education is wide and assumes receiving it by various means, it is also affirmed that the context of the two first sentences of the article should be interpreted as a reference to the education given in schools.[268] Subject to Article 41, the right to education may be invoked and claimed within the confines of laws. Therefore, the ordinary law has to materialise and particularise this right on the basis of the Czech constitutional order, as well as all the relevant international instruments that the Czech Republic is party of (Article 10 of the Constitution). The ordinary laws need to be framed in accordance to the provisions of Article 4 paras.2 and 4 of the Charter that subjects the limitations placed upon the fundamental rights and basic freedoms to the conditions prescribed in the Charter. It also requires that the essence and significance of these rights and freedoms is preserved. Art.4 para.4 explicitly says that "*(s)uch limitations are not to be misused for purposes other*

267 O. Rudak, *Prawo do nauki*, in: B. Banaszak, A. Preisner (eds.), *Prawa i wolności konstytucyjne obywateli RP*, Warszawa 2002, p.494-496.

268 V. Pavlíček (ed.), *Ústava a ústavní řád České republiky...*, p.264.

than those for which they were laid down".[269] The right to education is considered as a fundamental right, and as mentioned above, it is interpreted according to international standards given to this right mainly by the ICESCR of 16 December 1966, the International Covenant on the Rights of the Child of 20 November 1989, and the Protocol of the Convention for the Protection of Human Rights and Fundamental Freedoms of 20 March 1952. According to Art.33 para.2 the citizens have the right to free education at primary and secondary levels, and at university level depending on particular citizens' abilities and the capability of the society. It therefore expresses the obligation of the state to provide free public education on the first two levels, while setting a separate regime for the university level education.

The **Slovak Constitution** copied the formulation of the right to education from the Charter of Fundamental Rights and Basic Freedoms. Therefore, the doctrinal interpretation of Article 42 of the Slovak Constitution is very similar, if not identical to the Czech interpretation. The extent to which education in Slovakia is free is, first, limited by the provision indicating that it applies to citizens,[270] and second, that it applies in full to the elementary and secondary (high-school) level. Further, at the university level- education is restrained "depending on the abilities[271] of the individual and the potential of the society". The doctrine explains the latter reservation by referring to the two premises- objective and subjective. The objective premise (*objektívna podmienka*) assumes a possibility of putting pressure on the society and refers to the positive state action with respect to its financial ability to provide for adequate budgetary means for a system of free education. The subjective premise (*subjektívna podmienka*) relates to the personal ability of an individual to pursue education at the university level.

---

269 *Listina Základních Práv Svobod. Charter of Fundamental Rights and Basic Freedoms*, Brno 1997 (official English translation; copy with the author)

270 The doctrine points out a certain paradox in the text of the constitution. Taking under consideration the fact that Art.42 para.2 has the character of a specific standard that is linked to the financial aspect of ensuring the right to education, it may not be assumed that this right may be applicable to citizens only. Foreigners have a right to education guaranteed in Art.42 para.1. In what follows, constitutionalists interpret it as a constitutional inconsistency, which provides the right to education at university level only to those citizens who prove their ability to pursue education at university, whereas it does not grant similar reservation with respect to the foreigners. See: Ján Drgonec, *Základne práva a slobody podľ'a Ústavy Slovenskej republiky. Zväzok 2*, Manz, Bratislava 1999, p. 233.

271 The *schopnost* in the English official version of the Czech Charter is translated as *abilities*, whereas the Slovak version translates the same word as *capabilities*. See: *Listina Základních Práv Svobod. Charter of Fundamental Rights and Basic Freedoms*, Brno 1997, and the official version of English translation of the *Constitution of the Slovak Republic* (both copies with the author).

Most of the constitutional lawyers interpret this ability (*schopnost*) as the adequate competence of a candidate who wants to enter a university.[272] The reading of the first two paragraphs of Article 42 lead to the conclusion that there are two types of issues in relation to the university level education: the first concerns the right of an access to university education, and the second concerns the right to free university education.[273]

Both the Czech (Art.33 para.3 of the Charter)[274] and the Slovak (Art.42 para.3 of the Constitution) formulation of the right to education contain a provision granting the right to establish and to give instruction in other than public schools. The Slovak doctrine is rather moderate in interpretation of this provision, as it limits the elucidation of this paragraph to the statement that the education in such schools may be subject to tuition fees and that the conditions regulating establishment and instruction in non-public schools is subject to ordinary legislation.[275] The Czech doctrine develops the above by adding that the conditions established by statutes must guarantee equal quality of teaching as in public schools in order to allow choice individual can take in choosing a school, and to guarantee the possibility to pursue education on higher levels. It is asserted, therefore that the right guaranteed in Art.33 para.3 of the Charter is an exception given to the general rule, that is that the state provides free education at elementary and secondary levels.[276]

---

272 Ján Svák, Ľubor Cebulka, *Ústavné právo Slovenskej republiky. Vybrané otázky, teorie, výučby a praxe,* Bratislavská vysoká škola práva, 2006, p.176. It is also noticed that the abilities, such as appropriate level of knowledge and/or competences to enter university, which are subject to the internal regulation of a university, is only one element of the precondition to pursue education at the university level. The second element of this precondition is to be seen in the ability of the candidate to secure for him/herself appropriate financial means in order to be able to study at the university, i.e. administrative fees, the costs of academic books, or the costs of living in the place where the person is studying. Compare: Ján Drgonec, *Ústava Slovenskej republiky. Komentár,* Heuréka 2004, p.300; also: *The Opinion of the Conference of Rectors of Academic Schools in Poland on the SK 18/99 case* delivered to the Constitutional Tribunal , available at: www.krasp.org.pl

273 Ján Drgonec, *Ústava Slovenskej republiky...*, p.301.

274 The official English translation of the Article 33 para.3 says: „*Private schools may be established and instruction provided there only under conditions set by law; the education at such schools may be provided in exchange for tuition.*" The original version, however, uses the expression "*jiné školy než státní*", which should be rather translated as other than public instead of private.

275 Ján Drgonec, *op.cit.*, p.301.

276 V. Pavlíček (ed.), *op.cit.*, p.271.

Although the right to free education is explicitly stated in the three constitutions, its interpretation has nevertheless brought in many questions on what it means in the reality. The doubts arose especially in the context of the reduction of budgetary costs for education in the first years of transformation to market economy, or when contrasted with the sense of the free provision of education established within the communist regimes. At that time the government was paying all direct and most indirect costs of education. Consequently, the right to **free public education** on the primary and/or secondary level was subject of one of the earliest judgments of the three Constitutional Courts. The relevant complaints brought in the question of indirect violation of the right to free education in public schools.

In the judgment on entitlements to reduced transportation tickets for pupils and students[277] the Polish Constitutional Court referred to the question whether the introduction of the age limit for eligibility for discounted tickets for pupils and students infringed the right to free education. The Tribunal stated that although the introduction of the criterion of age in this case was not based on a logical rationale (the regulation lead to a *de facto* discrimination within a particular group of the society) and thus, violated the principle of social justice, its relationship with the right to free education was indirect and too remote. According to the Tribunal, the subject matter of the complaint fell under another constitutional notion, that is of "other forms of material assistance", the provision which obliged the state to take action. It must be noted in the margin that the Court referred in this case to the constitutional right of education as formulated in Article 72 para.2 of the 1952 Constitution as amended. The article in question did not provide for a subjective right, but was formulated as a policy goal.[278]

---

277 *K 3/94*

278 The Tribunal has also underlined elsewhere that because of the constitutional change, the insertion of new constitutional principles that have the nature of the *lex posterior* and thus are considered as chief principles (*zasady naczelne*), are in fact the leading principles. This is of primary importance to the interpretation of the rights maintained in the in force constitutional law. In light of the above, the content of the maintained rights must be understood as a catalogue of values that must be taken into account and protected in the materialisation of the principle of social justice through the state ruled by law (*demokratyczne państwo prawne*). Yet, both the guiding directives for the state and claim rights contained in this catalogue must be interpreted so that their materialisation does not collide with fulfilment of other constitutional values that constitute the principle of social justice and of the rule of law. In *K 21/95* judgment the Tribunal also addressed the question whether the reduction of age limit to 20 years of age for the entitlement to child benefit results in a legitimate differentiation of the situation of students. In its conclusions the Court stated that the issue of a financial support of the State to students is not a matter of a regulation through child benefit allowances, but of a comprehensive system of academic scholarships.

The right to free education in the Czech and Slovak constitutions was interpreted with the provision of free text books and school accessories falling within the right to free public education. The Czech Constitutional Court based its reasoning on a conviction that the costs resulting from the materialisation of the right to education could be divided between the state and the citizen. The Court argued that besides the obligation of the state to take positive action, it is in a citizen's own interest to obtain an education, and in this way also to gain higher qualifications and thus, as a result better opportunities on the labour market. The Court admitted that the expenses connected to the materialisation of the right to education were a long-term investment in the life of citizens, and that the state bore the major part of these costs. Yet, it does not follow from the previous information that the state was obliged to bear the entire cost.[279] Contrary to the Polish and Czech Constitutional Court, the Slovak Constitutional Court mostly based its argumentation on the grammatical interpretation of the word "free". Not only did the Slovak Court refer to international treaties but it also extensively used dictionaries in order to interpret the significance of the provision of free education.[280] It paid a lot of attention to the linguistic translation of the ICESCR, referring to both the English and French version of the particular provisions, and translating it into Slovak, or giving it the exact interpretation within the national law.

In the three preceeding cases, the Constitutional Courts had to define the scope of the right to free education, and indirectly set the limits of claims arising from its realisation. It is apparent from the above that although the three Constitutional Courts used different interpretative techniques, they reached the same conclusion, i.e. refused to admit wide ranging claim rights stemming from the realisation of the right to free education. The extensive and purposeful analysis of the Polish Court favoured the goals and aspirations expressed by the provision on the right to free education with reference to the constitutional principle of social justice and the principle of the state ruled by law. While the Polish Tribunal sought to distinguish the substance of the right to education from claim

279 *Pl. ÚS 25/94*

280 The Court referred to the definitions of a word "free" contained in: the Oxford Dictionary-Shorter, Webster's Third New International Dictionary, Littré: Dictionnaire de la langue française, Hatzfeld et Darmesteter Dictionnaire general de la langue française, and Larousse- Dictionnaire de la langue française. *PL. ÚS 5/93,* unpublished; copy with the author.

rights that led to its realisation,[281] the Czech and Slovak Courts decided to use the restrictive interpretation of the provision. The grammatical analysis narrowed down the focus of the latter two courts to the technical meaning of the words "free education" in the given constitutional provisions. With reference to the preceding text, it should be noticed that the Czech and Slovak Courts made little effort to implement their own constitutional provisions into the nascent democratic legal system. By a plain reference to the textual meaning of the right to free education these Courts abandoned the task of building up their legitimacy in adjudication on socio-economic matters.

As mentioned earlier, university education is governed by a separate regime. Not only does it introduce a competence based system of selection, but also subjects the provision of instruction on this level to the financial situation of the state. This is at least, how the Czech and Slovak constitutions frame it. The Polish case is more complex as it does not explicitly establish a separate system for university level education, although the rulings of the Constitutional Tribunal confirm this approach. Still, it was the question of the **free access to university education** that concerned the three Constitutional Courts.

The dispute over the conformity of tuition fees for studies with Article 70 para.2 brought by an individual complaint, was subject to the Polish Constitutional Court judgment number ***SK 18/99***.[282] The competence given to public higher institutions (universities) to impose fees for educational services other than teaching in full-time programs (i.e. part-time, evening and external studies) was confronted with the provision of free education in public schools and the exception that statutes may allow payments for certain services provided by public institutions of higher education. Although the complaint was found inadmissible for the constitutional review on the merits, the Tribunal has nevertheless addressed fundamental issues, thus clarifying the meaning of Art.70 para.2. In essence, the Court stated that the right to education, as provided in Art.70, entails the duty of the state to guarantee available and universal education. This is not corollary however to the idea of education free of charge.

281 In the early jurisprudence the Tribunal gave priority to newly established constitutional principles resulting from the rule of law, over the catalogue of the maintained rights. This was especially important with respect to the wide catalogue of social rights preserved, and then reformulated by the 1997 Constitution.

282 The Polish Constitutional Court judgment *SK 18/99* of 8 November 2000 on tuition fees for studies, Z.U.2000/7/258; Dz.U.2000.101.1091 of 23 November 2000.

The Polish constitutional doctrine links the right to education to the freedom of scientific research and freedom to teach (Article 73), as well as to the principle of impartiality in matters of personal conviction, whether religious or philosophical of public authorities, therefore also of schools (Article 25 para.2). It also provides for the right of parents to ensure their children a moral and religious upbringing in accordance with their convictions (Article 53 para.3), which is further connected to the acceptability of teaching religion in schools (Article 53 para.4).[283]

The issue of teaching religion in public schools exemplifies particularities of interpretation of equality and non-discrimination clauses in relation to the right of education. Two of the most significant cases on the teaching of religion (catechesis) in public schools delivered by the Constitutional Tribunal in the early 1990s, together with a case on the same subject from 2 December 2009, bring up numerous controversies, but most importantly touch upon the debate over the impartiality of the state towards religions versus the exclusion of religion of any kind from public sphere. In these cases, the state neutrality and impartiality towards religion clashes with the free exercise of religion and with the question to what extent the presence of religion in schools does or does not discriminate against non-religious individuals or minority religion believers. In chronological order, the cases revolved around such issues as: giving Churches and religious associations the possibility to use school class rooms; the equality of Churches and religious associations in the exercise of the privilege to teach religion in public schools; the inclusion of religion in the curriculum and on the graduation diplomas; the principle of free-will in participation in facultative classes (such as religion or ethics); the competences of the Minister of Education and of Churches in setting the teaching program and conditions of employment of teachers; and finally reckoning catechesis or ethics marks among all other marks when counting the average on graduation diplomas. A holistic vision of the right to education on the one hand and the reference to equality and non-discrimination clauses on the other is subject in Polish Constitutional Court rulings to the principle of the protection of Christian values. The two above mentioned principles are not given priority in the Tribunal's rulings. The reference to the protection of Christian values is given precedence over these principles and thus gives rise to the criticism of the "pliancy" of the Polish Constitutional Court.[284] The unilateral attitude of the Constitutional Tribunal is manifested in

283 Kazimierz Działocha, Paweł Sarnecki, Wojciech Sokolewicz, *Konstytucja Rzeczypospolitej Polskiej: Komentarz III*, Leszek Garlicki (ed.), Wydawnictwo Sejmowe, Warszawa, 2003, p.3.

284 Wojciech Sadurski, *Miętkość trybunalska*, Gazeta Wyborcza, 7 December 2009.

its selective approach to social facts. The Tribunal ascertains the privileged position of the Roman Catholic confession by admitting that the domination of the Roman Catholic religion catechesis in schools stems from the social fact of the predominance of the Roman Catholic confession in Poland.[285] By following a particular axiology, which is the unquestionable importance of the Christian upbringing for the society, the Constitutional Tribunal not only prioritises social facts over the rule of law, but moves towards subordination of the constitutional control to the principles of prevailing, officially approved religion.[286] From the analysis of the three rulings it stems that the principal arguments used by the Tribunal and repeated in the successive cases- that the teaching of religion in public schools is a manifestation of the freedom of religion, or that numerous international treaties and declarations bound Poland to ensure religious education to children- was developed into more and more fundamental statements, which instead of reflecting the entire legal complexity of the situation, show the inconsistency of the Tribunal's reasoning. Firstly, the reasons used in the earliest ruling are simply repeated in subsequent cases, but are not given careful consideration in order to provide for a coherent Court's argumentation. For instance, one of the main issues raised in the rulings concerned the legality of instructions (later: ministerial decrees), that is whether the concrete legal solution

285 For example, in the ruling K 11/90, the Constitutional Tribunal bases its arguments on relevant facts (actual situation) prior to the issuance of the instructions and refers to the absence of religion in schools under the communist regime. By stating that the previous political system have "illegally and dishonourably eliminated religious instruction from schools", it is assumed that bringing back religious instruction to public schools ensures the enforcement of the constitutional freedom of conscience and religion (Article 82, section 1 of the 1952 Constitution, as amended). This opinion is further strengthened by a reference to numerous international instruments that impose on the state the duty to ensure religious education. English summary of the ruling available at: http://www.trybunal.gov.pl/eng/Judical_Decisions/1986_1999/K_%2011_90a.pdf. The question of whether religious education has to be given in public schools remains dubious in this light, as well as dubious is the fact of the remuneration of religion teachers from public funds and full competence of Churches to define the curriculum and competences of the teachers. These issues were raised in the two dissenting opinions to the above mentioned ruling.

286 In the ruling *U 12/92*, the Tribunal states that the autonomy of both Church and State does not mean acting in isolation, but is seen as the possibility to cooperate to achieve a common goal, that is the "ethical education of youth". In *K 11/90* ruling the Tribunal claims that the State cannot evade of the duty to ensure religious education, even if Church institutions organise and provide for such an education by their own means. Compare with the Engel v. Vitale decision of the U.S. Supreme Court, which declared unconstitutional the inclusion of state-sponsored school prayer as a part of instruction in public schools. *Engel v. Vitale*, 370 U.S. 421 (1962).

could have been introduced by an instruction, or whether the subject matter had fallen under the statutory regulation. In both of the 1990s cases the Tribunal held that the Minister of Education had the right to regulate religious issues by means of a regulation, which went clearly against the Tribunal's own established precedent on the legislative authority.[287] In these highly controversial cases the Tribunal did not present a coherent justification for its decision mainly due to political pressures.[288] It preferred to refer to the commonly recognised social facts where a particular argument served to support the recognition of the dominant position of Roman Catholic confession, therefore, for example the Tribunal pointed in its reasoning to the obligations stemming from the realisation of international human rights treaties in order to strengthen its arguments.[289] It also stressed numerous reservations of the ministerial instruction, which stated that a common prayer in a classroom (which constitutes an element of the catechesis) requires special attention and discretion in order not to offend the religious feelings of non-believers or minority believers. It held firmly, on the other hand, its competence to review laws only when the social facts seemed to depart from the envisaged equality and non-discrimination of religions. For instance by saying that the instructions in no way restrict the teaching of religion to Christian confessions, even though the Tribunal itself noticed (but not recognised) that the

287 The earlier case law established that the executive branch may issue implementing regulations (by instructions, or later ministerial decrees) only if expressly authorized to do so by the delegation clauses of parliamentary statutes, and thus those administrative decisions that go beyond their statutory authorisation are unconstitutional. See for example: Judgment *U 5/86* of 5 November 1986, where the Tribunal said that the Council of Ministers did not receive any statutory delegation to extend the rules of determining the costs of maintenance and repairs laid for individuals who bought their apartments rather than rented them from the state. The Court expressly stated that "a statutory delegation is always subject to a strict and literal interpretation; assuming that a delegation comprises matters not enumerated in it on the grounds, for instance, of a teleological interpretation is, as a rule, out of question." English summary of the case available at: http://www.trybunal.gov.pl/eng/Judical_Decisions/1986_1999/U_%2005_86a.pdf

288 Also the pressure of the Catholic Church representatives was of significance for the failure of the Tribunal to follow its precedent on the legislative authority. The story revealed after some time by the then-Ombudsman shows that only three out of six dissenting justices decided to write their decisions down and enclose it to the judgment, thus revealing their names. After: Agnieszka Klich, *Human Rights in Poland: The Role of the Constitutional Tribunal and The Commissioner for Citizen's Rights*, St. Louis-Warsaw Transatlantic Law Journal 33, 1996.

289 The Tribunal stated that the instructions "provide for an organisational framework for all interested parties to express their opinion on the opportunity for teaching religion brought about the statute. [And that] this opportunity follows from natural and inalienable human rights and freedoms, which has already found expression in international law". See: English summary of the *K 11/90* ruling, p.6

instruction admits the possibility of displaying crosses or of saying prayers before and after every class, the provisions that explicitly introduce such a possibility did not originate from instructions but were established by Article 15, section 2 of the Act of 17 May 1989 on the Relationship of the State to the Roman Catholic Church.[290] Secondly, the inconsistency of the Tribunal's reasoning is manifested in the attitude to the inconsistencies of laws. The controversy arose when the Tribunal first stated in the ***K 11/90*** judgment that the particular provisions of the Act of 15 July 1961 on the Development of the System of Education[291] contravene the principles defined in the Act of 17 May 1989 on the Relationship of the State to the Catholic Church, and thus according to the *lex posterior derogat legi priori* principle the former provisions were to be considered as not applicable to the case. Two weeks later it issued a signalling decision,[292] in which it advised the Parliament to take the necessary steps to pass a new law that would reflect the current political and legal reality. This inconsistency proves the lack of courage of the Court to address the legal discrepancies in the case itself. In the ***U 12/92*** judgment, the Court largely omitted the rule subjecting the teaching of religion to the competences of Churches and shifted the entire responsibility to the Minister of Education. It thus, over-interpreted the existing law in order to strengthen the precedence it established in the ***K 11/90*** judgment on the "predestination" of the State to provide for religious education. Consequently, the same reason was used in the ***U 10/07*** judgment on the inclusion of the religion or ethics marks on the graduation diplomas.

The Czech constitutional doctrine links the right to education at the university level to Art.15 para.2 to the freedom of thought, scholarly research and of artistic creation. It is apparent that the link is explicitly made with respect to the universities, and not to primary nor secondary schools.[293] It is claimed that from the point of view of state limits the specificity of the right to education is shaped according to the level at which the education is provided. Therefore, since universities are scholarly places of work (*vědecký pracoviště*) their connection to the provisions on the freedom of thought and scholarly research is greater than at other levels of education. The right to education, contrary to the Polish case,

---

290 *The Act of 17 May 1989 on the Relationship of the State to the Roman Catholic Church*, Journal of Laws, Number 29, Item 154, amended by the Journal of Laws, 1990, Number 51, Item 297. The reasoning of the Court used in *K 11/90* judgment.

291 *The Act of 15 July 1961 on the Development of the System of Education*, Journal of Laws, Number 32, Item 160 as amended

292 *S 1/91* of 13 February 1991, Signalling Decision concerning the case K 11/90 of 30 January 1991, Z.U. 1991// 29; OTK 1986-1995/t3/1991/29.

293 V. Pavlíček (ed.), *Ústava a ústavní řád České Republiky...* p.268.

is not directly linked to the freedom of thought as provided for in para.1 of Article 15, that is to the freedom of thought, conscience and religious conviction.[294]

In light of the presented cases, the Polish Tribunal Court seemed to give precedence to the doctrinal claim that the duty of the state is to provide for and organise education. Nevertheless, the precedence given to this particular duty of the state and simultaneous marginalisation of equality and anti-discrimination provisions proves that the Court went contrary to the fundamental purpose of constitutional rights, which is to impose limits upon majoritarian decisions in the political process. This is why the position of the Constitutional Tribunal is exposed to criticism for the lack of judicial consistency with respect to the rule of law and intentions to protect human rights. The judgements cited above illustrate the example of where bureaucratic arbitrariness and general lack of human rights awareness perpetuate abuse. The power of democracy lies in its defence of the rights of the majority, but its weakness involves a danger of discrimination of the rights of minorities. Even more the fallacy of democracy stands, when the majority uses its position to overrule the minority and to influence the judicial or independent control bodies such as Ombudsmen. The Polish Tribunal has proven itself open to many of the Commissioner's arguments having a natural law basis. The static nature of the Constitutional Tribunal contrasted with the naturalist character of the Commissioner, most clearly visible in the cases of religion and abortion. Yet, the issues of religion and abortion are among the most controversial of all social issues in many parts of the world. They involve difficult individual choices that no law can fully control. Still, judicial inconsistency is hardly acceptable when it comes to building foundations for a state that is subject to the rule of law and intends to protect human rights. In this context a number of systemic and institutional limitations that make it uncertain whether the office of the Commissioner and the Tribunal have fully succeeded in generating the "secondary rules" necessary to guarantee human rights in Poland may be observed.[295] Economic difficulties jeopardize economic and social rights. The euphoria of democracy has led to democratic populism which tends to neglect the rights of minorities. Political pressure has led to problematic decisions in cases involving religious instruction and abortion.

294 In the commentary to the Charter a mention is made to a change that concerned the interpretation of the freedom of scholarly research at the statutory level. The Higher Education Act No.172/1990 interpreted the freedom of scholarly research inter alia as a right to various philosophical and religious beliefs, and a right to promote them. The Act on Higher Education No.11/1998 already changed this interpretation referring only to the freedom of knowledge, research and artistic creation, as well as to publishing its outcomes. See: V. Pavlíček (ed.), *op.cit.*, p.166-168.

295 Agnieszka Klich, *op.cit.*

A general observation that emerges from these reflections is that the more controversial the case, the more axiological argument is used. There is indeed a need to explain the controversies, but if the legal component is under-developed in such reasoning, the overall ruling is poor, weekly grounded and not entirely reliable. Moreover, the Constitutional Court exposes itself to the danger by compulsorily persisting in its earlier decisions regardless the complexity of *ad casum* character of constitutional cases. It is worth noting that in cases concerning the interpretation of the notion of social justice, the Polish Constitutional Court is moderate and reserved. It prefers to find the questioned laws as unconstitutional, when infringement of determined constitutional principles are evident and unquestionable. It uses a different attitude, however, with respect to the cases where the dilemmas concern issues connected to the philosophy of life, such as conscience and religion.

PART III

PROTECTION AND PROMOTION OF SOCIAL AND ECONOMIC RIGHTS. EXCLUSSIVENESS VERSUS INCLUSSIVENESS OF DIFFERENT STATE ACTORS

Chapter 6
Inter-Institutional Constitutional Dialogue in Socio-Economic Cases

Contrary to prevailing views, the contents of fundamental rights are not defined solely by constitutional courts. It is true that the aspect of constitutional justiciability renders significant powers to constitutional courts in this respect. But the very principle of democracy the separation of powers principle establishes a rule of the balance of powers among constitutional organs. It is therefore the three branches- the legislative, the executive and the judiciary- that are responsible for giving an effect to constitutional provisions, those concerning socio-economic rights included. The difficulty in deciding who decides, however remains unresolved, largely due to the fact that the constitutions do not precisely specify the ultimate power of any of the institutions to give the final interpretation of the constitution. It is often the case that constitutional courts are considered to give the final opinions on the compatibility of laws of a lower rank (like statutes, acts of law) with the constitution. Thus, in a way, the courts judge the performance of the legislature and/or the executive. Yet, it is still up to the legislator to reverse, modify or void the court' decisions which invalidates legislation, and therefore, achieve their social or economic policy ends.

Consequently, the dual nature of the judicial role in adjudicating on constitutional cases proves the complexity of the question under consideration. One common belief is that the constitutional judge is regarded as a protector and determiner of rights. In this conviction, the judge's role is evaluated in terms of a classical understanding of judicial functions. It presupposes, that a judge has a final say over the constitutionality, and thus, the fairness of the statutory rules and regulations. A second, very different mode of conceptualizing the role of the judge- and especially of the constitutional judge- is based on a conviction that the judge's role is brought to the function of an arbiter, who decides in cases resulting from the ambiguity of the dispersion of governmental powers within the horizontal and vertical dependences of the governance systems. It is indeed a matter of controversy whether judges strive to make principled decisions according to constitutional laws or principles,[296] or whether they decide on technicalities, allowing the elected bodies to "correct their mistake". To make matters more complicated, the judge's two functions often overlap, as one cannot really deny either the influential constitutional decisions or the rulings that are close to law-making, nor can one deny the judge's attempts to stay away from politics and leave a margin of discretion to the legislator, especially within the field of social and economic rights.[297]

In a broader sense, the question of institutional choice, although unspecified in constitutions, is implicitly left to the judiciary. At the same time, however, while the court asserts its constitutional power to decide who decides, it constantly recognises its ultimate reliance on these branches of state authorities that enforce its decisions and rulings. The difficulty arises with the fact that simultaneously court needs to protect their independence and autonomy from the executive and legislative actors. Therefore, the question concerns the political culture rather than a particular legal solution. The way in which the court allocates the power to decide- either by granting such a prerogative to itself, or shifting it to the other state actors- enforces its position and legitimacy to ultimately decide who decides. But the space determined by the court, in which the power of constitutional politics may be institutionally consolidated,[298] gives only a partial answer to the existing problem. This is why, if a particular constitutional case is to find a decent solution in a given time, the dialogue between the institutions is needed.

The dialogue between the court and decision-making institutions, however, does not depend on a case and should not be assigned to a particular case or a problem. In light of this the intra-institutional constitutional dialogue is understood as a constant channelling of information between the court and the legislature, and/or other constitutional actors. The information on existing assumptions, state capacities, policy guidelines accepted by the government, the ability to render feasibility to the court's decisions are a substance of such dialogue. Institutions therefore, need to find a way to channel this information in seeking for a solution to the constitutional controversy. In this way, constitutional politics

---

296 Another problem for discussion appears in this place: the problem of the vagueness of the constitutional principles allowing constitutional judges to enter into deliberations on law and morals. For the sake of the consistency of the main argument on institutional dialogue, this very interesting and intricate question remains consciously omitted.

297 Hans Klug, *op.cit.,* p.188.

298 Hans Klug, *op.cit.*

should be seen as a careful deliberation of political interests on one hand, and of constitutional premises on the other hand. Moreover, the intra-institutional dialogue should be based on mutual respect. It is not only the court who deliberates on political interests, but also politicians who should deliberate on constitutional foundations.

6.1 The Theory of Constitutional Dialogue

The notion of judicial review understood as a "dialogue" between judges and legislatures has its origins in the article by two Canadian scholars- Peter Hogg and Allison Thornton.[299] The dialogue metaphor is most commonly used to describe the courts and the legislatures' interactions in the determination of the "proper balance between constitutional principles and public policies".[300] It has nevertheless, been extended to embrace a wider spectrum of actors who are involved in the constitutional decision-making- such as ordinary and supreme courts, Ombudsmen, administrative agencies, etc. The dialogue theory therefore comprises of a set of interfaces mostly between constitutional bodies, and relates not only to the translation of the constitutional courts' decisions to legislative process, but also to their transmission to the decisions of ordinary courts and administrative agencies. The notion of constitutional dialogue, as used here, is understood as an intra-institutional dialogue only, and does not take into account any form of "personal dialogue" that takes place between judges themselves when they seek inspiration for their reasoning and/or final decisions.

There are two major factors that influence the materialisation the dialogue between Constitutional Courts and other institutions that shape the laws. First, is the vision of the constitutional rights. Second, is thc vision of judicial review, that is the competences granted to Constitutional Courts, and the institutional setting within which they operate. These factors however, are subject to interpretation of all actors in the dialogue. It means, that it is not only the interpretation of constitutional rights performed by the Constitutional Courts that is at stake. What also counts is the role and importance given to these rights by the rest of the participants in the dialogue. Likewise, the position of the Constitutional Courts within this network is not only shaped by the self-positioning of

299 Peter Hogg and Alison Thornton (Bushell) in Peter W. Hogg, Allison A. Bushell, *The Charter Dialogue Between Courts and Legislatures (Or Perhaps the Charter of Rights Isn't Such A Bad Thing After All)*, 35 Osgoode Hall Law Journal 75 (1997).

300 Luc B. Tremblay, *The legitimacy of judicial review: The limits of dialogue between courts and legislatures*, I•CON, Volume 3, Number 4, 2005, pp.617-618, p.617.

these courts in the legal system, but again seeks for mutual recognition of all the parties of the dialogue. Furthermore, the constitutional dialogue is not a zero-sum condition. It is not a debate one must necessarily win or loose. Rather it is a process of rational persuasion, where arguments of all sides of the dispute are being expressed and exposed to a critical analysis.

In this perspective the constitutional dialogue is often described as an ongoing process of interaction, mostly between the courts and legislatures. It is based on the assumptions that while the courts are empowered with a competence to invalidate legislation on the basis of their own formal or substantive understanding of constitutional principles, the legislatures may reverse, modify or avoid their decisions. Accordingly, the courts are not granted the privilege of the final word over the balance between constitutional rights and state policies, as they are not the only actors who are eligible to give meaning to the constitution.[301] In the former view, the constitutional dialogue takes two forms: one of deliberation, or one of conversation. The dialogue as deliberation is not seen as "a veto over the politics"[302], but rather as a process that enhances democracy through a "public debate" in which constitutional values are given prominent consideration.[303] The public debate is the crux of the matter, as the dialogue understood as deliberation aims at agreeing a decision and collectively determining the most justified or optimal solution to a problem. In short, the deliberative form of the constitutional dialogue seeks to make collective decisions, settle practical conflicts and reach binding agreements. On the other hand, under the form of the conversation the dialogue is viewed as a process where the two actors perform their distinct but complementary roles. They enter into a continuous conversation which does not necessarily aim at solving a specific constitutional controversy, but in fact provides for a long term platform where views are exchanged. In the previous view, the case of the probable implementation of constitutional conceptions on the legal order as understood and enforced by the courts, may

301 The critics of constitutional dialogue theory condition it upon clear recognition of legislatures as legitimate interpreters of the constitution, who have effective means to assert that interpretation. This form of the constitutional dialogue corresponds to the theory of "coordinate construction". See: Kent Roach, *Constitutional and Common Law Dialogues. Between the Supreme Court and Canadian Legislatures*, 80 Canadian Bar Review (Can. Bar. Rev.) 481, 2001, p.529; Mark Tushnet, *Judicial Activism or Restraint in a Section 33 World*, 52 University of Toronto Law Journal, 2003.

302 Hogg and Bushell, *op.cit.*, p.105.

303 Hogg and Bushell, *op.cit.*, p.79.

only be verified in the long run, and is an empirical question of fact.[304] The division of the two concepts of constitutional dialogue in either a deliberation or a conversation was proposed by Luc Tremblay, who has further elaborated upon the limits of the theory of deliberative institutional dialogue. Tremblay argued that institutional dialogue in its form of deliberation is limited by two premises: *primo* by the doctrine of judicial responsibility, and *secundo* by the normative and conceptual aspect of the theory. The doctrine of judicial responsibility emphasizes the issue of judicial independence in the sense that, they must not subordinate their own convictions and practical judgments to the will of others. Assuming that deliberation seeks compromise in the final decision on the constitutionality of the legislation in question, this form of constitutional dialogue is burdened with the risk of becoming a political dialogue, while indeed dialogic theories should not be confused with judicial deference.[305] Yet, Tremblay concluded that in fact the dialogue understood as conversation, better addresses an adequate representation of courts and legislatures. Christine Bateup forwards a more general perspective and addressed the issue of the applicability of dialogic theory in practice. The context of this concern stems from the fact that the theory of constitutional dialogue principally did not operate in practice, but was rather viewed as a normative ideal.[306]

J.H. Ely's theory in turn assumed that courts' main role is to guard the process of democratic representation, and to prevent incumbent or powerful political actors from seizing full supremacy. His representation-reinforcing theory confines the judicial role to improving the democratic processes. The judicial role, as Ely conceived it, was to ensure that the legislation that comes from the political process can in fact reflect popular demands or visions. This contradicts the legislation seen as a product of bargaining at the expense of others which

304 Luc B. Tremblay, *op.cit.*, p.648. Tremblay explains it in the following way: "(…) *each institution is entitled to stick with its particular set of judgments and concerns; the courts may enforce the constitution as they understand it, and the legislatures will remain free to realize their original objectives, and, for that matter, by way of the original legislative means, all in accordance with their own understanding of constitutional requirements. (...) Consequently, a dialogue as a conversation (....) constitutes a social and political fact, namely, that the two institutions, disagreeing over the proper constitutional balance, exchange words, ideas, opinions, judgments, and experiences within a space of intersubjective meaning and institutional setting but without a specific commitment to reach practical mutual agreement.*" at p.644-645.

305 Luc B. Tremblay, *op.cit.*, p.634-638.

306 Christine Bateup, *The Dialogic Promise. Assessing the Normative Potential of Theories of Constitutional Dialogue*, Brook. L. Rev., Vol. 71 Issue 3, 2006, pp.1109-1180, p.1121-1122.

was performed among limited interest groups.[307] In light of this, the judicial review should protect the *basic infrastructure of liberal democracy* [emphasis added]- rights of assembly, debate and free elections. Therefore, no citizen ought to be excluded from participation in the process of collective debate and argument except on compelling grounds.[308] While the protection of the infrastructure of the democracy is indeed a fundamental precondition for the constitutional review to ensure the observance of the principal rules of the democratic system of law-making and democratic participation, the most articulated caveat when speaking about civic participation concerns reservations that stem from the application of the dialogue theory to socio-economic rights viewed as claim rights. These reservations assert that the dialogue between courts and legislators intensifies and exposes political disputes rather than addressing a proper and concrete constitutional question. Nevertheless, citizens' "participation in the process of collective debate" within the judicial review, should be seen in this respect as an expression made known to the rest of the participants in the dialogue. In this sense, citizens can voice their arguments but remain within the constraints of the conversation-dialogue type. Moreover, the perception of civic participation in the law-making process through direct exposure of political interests is mistaken and gives a simplified picture of the law-making process. In what follows, Ely's theory is close to what Patrick Monahan had argued with respect to a right of equal access to and participation in the political process. Monahan's assessment of the Canadian constitutional tradition emphasizes the democratic conception of constitutional review. He sees the judicial review as being conducted in the name of democracy, rather than as means of guaranteeing "right answers" to the political, it is a mechanism to protect existing opportunities for democratic debate.[309] In this sense civic participation is also expressed by the representative role of the Parliament as the legislator, whose position leads to the promotion of people's involvement in the law-making process.

Notwithstanding, the variety of inter-connections within the actors of this conversation, it is important to keep in mind that the dialogue metaphor refers rather to the idea of intra-institutional deliberation on the given matters, and its

307 See generally: John Hart Ely, *Democracy and Distrust. A Theory of Judicial Review*, Harvard University Press, 1980.

308 John Hart Ely, *op.cit.*, p.124.

309 Patrick Monahan, *Politics and the Constitution: The Charter, Federalism and the Supreme Court of Canada,* Carswell, Scarborough 1987. Monahan stresses the tradition of promotion of people's capacity for self-government. In this light, the judicial review is opposed to the idea that it serves to circumscribe and bypass the political process. .After: Christopher P. Manfredi, Mark Rush (eds.), *Judging Democracy*……., p.28.

function is a contribution to the ongoing debate over the democratic legitimacy of judicial review.

The theory of constitutional dialogue, however, comprises an important element, which perhaps is shadowed by the dominance of the institutional aspect in the legal literature. The constitutional dialogue is preconditioned by either an *inherent and direct* or *external and indirect* duty of the dialogue's participants to deal with the constitution. It means that all the actors of the constitutional dialogue are bound by the provisions of the constitution and are obliged to fulfil it. Such a statement is trivial perhaps at a first glance, as it is obvious that all institutions are bound by the constitution. Nevertheless, the ability of entering into constitutional dialogue requires institutions to perform a long-term, constitutional thinking. What is called here the *inherent and direct* interpretation of the constitution refers to the function of constitutional court, which *de lege* is called to ensure the respect of constitutional provisions mostly through ruling on the validity of secondary law. On the other hand the *external and indirect* interpretation of the constitution refers to these institutions that in spite of being bound by the constitution are deemed to perform its tasks and duties in a constitutional, long-term perspective. This observation stems from the noticeable fact that notwithstanding their constitutional duties, the law-makers in the three countries under research, are most often than not guided by a short-term perspective of their law-making function, which is most likely far from being compatible with constitutional vision of materialisation of the rule of law, or particular constitutional rights. Therefore, a constitutional thinking is an indispensable element of the constitutional dialogue.

The bias towards materialisation of constitutional provisions is reflected by the references to the constitution in the legislative process and in the construction of the legal act itself. It is not equivalent to the interpretation of the constitution by the law-maker or other actors of the dialogue, certainly in the light of the centralised system of constitutional review. The crux of the matter therefore lies in the long-term constitutional reflection and creation of a comprehensive and complete systems of laws.[310] The picture is completed by the fact that the procedures of law-making in the countries under study here, tend to rely not only on

310 Yet in quite different perspective Mark Tushnet addressed the issue of legislatures enacting statutes without discussing constitutional norms. Tushnet defined the problem of a "democratic debilitation" in the context of reluctance of the legislatures to take up the task of referring to the constitution, but instead relying on the courts who consider constitutional dilemmas of a given piece of legislation . See: Mark Tushnet, *Policy Distortion and Democratic Debilitation: Comparative Illumination of the Countermajoritarian Difficulty,* Michigan Law Review, Vol. 94, No.2, 1995, pp.245-301.

a short-term perspectives and lack a holistic constitutional approach of the legislative process, but also of the implementations of laws.[311] Moreover, the dialogue theory in this aspect seeks to facilitate a broader constitutional debate over constitutional controversies that arise either from the action of courts or any other participant of the dialogue. This happening through drawing the attention of different interest groups of the society, contributes to shaping the content of the debate in the view of educating all the actors not only on diverging opinions or convictions, but more importantly in the view of leading to possible modification of various positions and further constitutional challenge over time as parties re-adapt their views.[312]

The fusion of an ultra-institutional element, that is the actual consciousness of institutional actors of their participation in the dialogue, into the intra-institutional dialogue theory holds the potential to address the actual problem of a more comprehensive understanding of different institutional and social aspects of constitutional dialogue.

---

311 In Poland for instance the evaluation of the compatibility of the law-making process with the long-term constitutional reflection of its provisions therein emerges rather as a wish than reality. It is claimed that the Polish Parliament is more concentrated on the short-term goals directed to addressing current affairs. The lack of strategic reflection, especially as to the results of the laws results in an inconsistent legal system. Moreover, the reliance on the interest groups and unclear lobbying procedures escalate the perception of the legal system as floating and depending on particular interests of a given political party. Additionally, the instability of the party system contributes to vague role of long-term strategic thinking, also in terms of constitutional compatibility. See for example: Wiesław Staśkiewicz, *Stanowienie prawa*, in: Lena Kolarska-Bobińska (ed.), *Co warto, co należy zmienić? Poprawa jakości demokracji w Polsce*, Instytut Spraw Publicznych, Warszawa 2008; Wiesław Staśkiewicz, *Prawo jako narzędzie polityki państwa okresu przemian (przeszłość wobec przyszłości)*, in: Marek Zubik (ed.), *Prawo a polityka*, Liber, Warszawa 2007.

312 In fact, one of the critics of the coordinate construction theory, Barry Friedman pointed out to a more substantive role of the (constitutional) court in the constitutional dialogue by claiming that to a large extent judicial decisions have served to further constitutional debates of a variety of actors. The debates served mutual recognition of diverging positions and produced answers over time that broadly conform to the preferred understanding of the constitution. See: Barry Friedman, *Dialogue and Judicial Review,* Michigan L. Rev., No. 91, 1993.

6.1.1 General Account of the *Inter-Institutional Dialogue* and the *Last Word* Theories

The central issue of the dialogue metaphor is not its design but its aim. Most importantly the dialogue theory assumes that a court decision on a contested issue is not regarded as a final judgment on the matter but as "a judicial invitation of further conversation- a kind of democratic dialogue- with legislatures and society".[313]

The most recent analysis of the performance of the Polish Constitutional court, conducted by constitutional scholars in the framework of the Ernst and Young study on good governance, stipulates a simple relationship by saying: the greater the impact of the Constitutional Courts decisions on ordinary courts rulings and legislature's decisions, the greater protection of constitutional rights, freedoms and of the constitutional regime as such.[314] At first glace, the approach to this rapport appears both consistent and unproblematic. Given that the Constitutional Courts verbalise the correct application of constitutional order in a given sphere of rights (civil and political, socio-economic) and refrain to take up the role of the negative legislator, it should be deemed that the fulfilment of its instruction provides for a comprehensive realisation of the constitutional order, including a proper materialisation of rights and freedoms contained therein. When this condition is met, one may talk about the desired situation: the *constitutional acquis* expressed in the theory of rights and freedoms, and in the interpretation of constitutional principles becomes applicable by other actors who participate in the creation of the domestic legal order (the courts, legislative bodies, administrative bodies, and agencies). However, an undisputed convergence in the sense of the influence of the constitutional adjudication on the following law-making processes is rare indeed.

Paraphrasing general observations of Manfredi and Rush, who addressed the theory of the constitutional dialogue in the context of the US Constitution and the Canadian Bill of Rights, in order to adjudicate challenges to given laws, the courts must come up with clear definitions of the rights at stake. This, in absence of a clear formulation of constitutional socio-economic provisions, leaves the

313 Ran Hirschl, *Canada's Contribution to the Comparative Study of Rights and Judicial Review*, in: Linda A. White, Richard Simeon (eds.), *The Comparative Turn in Canadian Political Scene*, UBC Press, 2008, p.84.

314 Tomasz Stawecki, Wiesław Staśkiewicz, Jan Winczorek, *Between Polycentrism and Fragmentation. The impact of Constitutional Tribunal Rulings on the Polish Legal Order*, Ernst and Young, Warsaw 2008.

Courts a wide margin of interpretation. Yet, the Courts ought to restrain from legislative attempts when defining these rights and placing them in the concrete policy context. However, if the Courts are too deferential, they risk enabling the legislatures to ground themselves in the monopoly of power, despite, of or at the expense of the political accountability of the elected officials.[315] Using the exact words of Manfredi and Rush, "[i]nsofar as there are many aspects of democratic theory, a court cannot justify imposing one particular democratic vision precisely because the people (and their elected representatives) might prefer yet equally justifiable vision of democracy."[316] In its pure form, this omits one important reservation: the idealistic assumption that the constitutional courts bear the privilege of the last word and thus shape domestic policies. Taking this proviso into account, the theory of constitutional dialogue seems to address the difficult reality of the materialisation of constitutional rights and freedoms, and especially of socio-economic constitutional provisions. In fact, much of the realisation of constitutional rights and freedoms may be attained through careful deliberation that is vital to democratic constitutionalism. In this light, the Courts are put in a difficult situation. On the one hand, they must remain a mainstay for constitutional standards and resist political and/or social pressures. On the other hand, again turning to the words of Manfredi and Rush "[t]o impose one democratic vision upon the political process would not only interfere with the legislative process but also risk debilitating the polity's capacity to deliberate and develop its capacity of self-government".[317]

Consensus building has both positive and negative aspects, as does democracy. Methods of constitutional interpretation guarantee equal participation of majorities and minorities. The assumption of judicial finality is in fact incorrect. With respect to constitutional decisions, while a judicial decision is final in the sense that it binds the parties to the action, it is rarely the final word in relation to the broader constitutional issues being considered due to a variety of institutional and political constraints on the Court. Enforcement is not automatic. So it could be said that judicial decrees do not necessarily constitute the final word in a particular case. The political branches of government can, and frequently do challenge judicial decision by enacting new legislation that tests or attempts to restrict court rulings.[318]

---

315 Christopher P. Manfredi, Mark Rush (eds.), *Judging Democracy……..*, p.13.

316 Christopher P. Manfredi, Mark Rush (eds.), *ibid.*

317 Christopher P. Manfredi, Mark Rush (eds.), *Judging Democracy……..*, p.13.

318 Christine Bateup, *The Dialogic Promise…*, p.1118-1119.

6.2 The Vision of Socio-Economic Constitutional Dialogue- Country Perspectives

It is commonly believed that in a democracy envisioning of constitutional rights directly relates to the performance of the regime. The example of the American constitutional tradition, which promotes individual rights and places substantive restrictions on the capacity of government to legislate, is often contrasted by a less individualistic European constitutional tradition. Yet, national constitutional traditions vary as to the interpretation of the constitutional rights, and especially as to the meaning given to constitutional socio-economic rights.

The theory of constitutional dialogue, developed in Canada, and then applied also in the US constitutional doctrine, gains more and more attention with respect to the constitutional adjudication in socio-economic matters of the Constitutional Court of the Republic of South Africa. Below, both elements of constitutional rights and of constitutional review are given attention in the researched country perspective. Not only are the considerations based on the Polish, Czech and Slovak constitutional doctrine and jurisprudence, but also the analysis is directly limited to the vision and interpretation of respectively, socio-economic rights and constitutional review in these matters. The following is a summarizing account of the dialogue theory juxtaposed with the last word theory.

Taking into consideration the fact, that the Polish Tribunal was set up and started its work under a pre-democratic era, the differences in its competences and methods of adjudication, as contrasted with these of the Czech or Slovak Constitutional Courts, are better explained. First, as a result of the granted competences, the decisions of the Polish Constitutional Courts for eleven years were not final. The Sejm could overrule any decision of the Tribunal it deemed contrary to its policy. Even the separation of the two Republics, and thus the following "division" of the Federal Constitutional Court into two separate national Constitutional Courts did not have any significant transposition to the Courts competences.[319] Second, in its early days the Polish Tribunal operated under the

319 The Constitutional Court of the Czechoslovak Federation was active for eleven months (from 31 January until 31 December 1992). During this time it has considered 1032 out of 1128 cases. After the Federation was annulled, the Court suspended 96 cases, and re-directed 34 cases to the Constitutional Court of the Slovak Republic, and 62 cases to the Constitutional Court of the Czech Republic, subjecting the re-direction of the cases to the relevant courts to the actual appointment of these Courts. See: Karel Klima, *La justice constitutionelle en Republique tchéque*, in: Marc Verdussen, *La justice constitutionnelle en Europe centrale. Centre d'études constitutionnelles et administratives, Bruxelles, Paris,* 1997 p.197

constitutional provisorium, which required it performed the exercise of the interpretation of the substance of the constitutional provisions from the beginning of its actions. Contrary to this, the Czech and Slovak Courts started to adjudicate under entirely changed constitutions. There were of course provisions reminiscent of the old constitutional system, such as the catalogue of rights. Nevertheless, the constitutional principles the two Constitutions contained were already based on the rule of law principle, and did not require the Court to provide for interpretative bridges, as was the Polish practice- in explaining the substance of a given right. This in turn, gave the Courts the comfort of not entering much into adjudicative practice in deliberations on the substance of the constitutional rights. It well explains why decisions of the two courts are rather short and concise in comparison with the decisions by the Polish Tribunal. Especially it is so, when comparing the early decisions of the three Courts.

With the introduction of the 1997 Constitution the competences of the Polish Tribunal were changed. Ever since the decisions of the Tribunal are final and universally binding. The Tribunal can prolong a date until the end of the biding force of a normative act until 18 months, and where a judgement has financial consequences not provided for in the budget it may seek for the opinion of the Council of Ministers (Art. 190 para.3 of the Constitution). The latter foundation is a premise for the institutional channelling of the constitutional dialogue. Previously the inter-institutional dialogue was initiated by provisions of the Constitutional Tribunal Act,[320] in the Statutes of the Sejm[321] and the Senate,[322] where respective articles set up the institutional framework for the dialogue between these bodies, and where the dialogue was based on the Court-legislature axis. According to Article 4.1 of the Constitutional Tribunal Act the Tribunal informs the Sejm and Senate about "The Substantial Problems Arising from the Activities and Judgments of the Tribunal".[323] Indeed it is a

320 The Constitutional Tribunal Act of 1 August 1997, Dz.U. No. 102, item, 643 with further amendments. English translation available at: www.trybunal.gov.pl/eng

321 Regulamin Sejmu Rzeczypospolitej, Uchwała Sejmu Rzeczypospolitej Polskiej z dnia 30 lipca 1992r, Mon. Pol. 2002, Nr. 23, poz. 398, ze zmianami, in: *Konstytucja Rzeczypospolitej Polskiej, Ustawa o Trybunale Konstytucyjnym...*, Wolters Kluwer Polska, Zakamycze, 2006, pp.253-330.

322 Regulamin Senatu, Uchwała Senatu Rzeczypospolitej Polskiej z dnia 23 listopada 1990r., Mon. Pol. 2002, Nr.54, poz.742 ze zmianami, available at: http://www.senat.gov.pl/senatrp/ustawy/regulami/regulamin.pdf

323 Once a year the Tribunal prepares a report *The Substantial Problems Arising from the Activities and Judgments of the Tribunal.* The document is accessible to the public and constitutes proper information sent to the "competent law-making bodies". The practice shows however, that the main addressees of the information are the both Chambers of the Parliament.

fact, that the yearly speeches of the President of the Constitutional Court in the Parliament became a practice, and that both the members of the parliament of the lower chamber, as well as the Senators, have the possibility to acquaint themselves with the most pertinent issues arising from the judicial practice of the Court. This is however, a first step to the dialogue, since so far these debates take rather a form of a monologue, rather than a proper conversation.[324]

Further, Article 4.2 of the Constitutional Tribunal Act states that "*the Tribunal shall submit to the competent law-making bodies observations concerning found inconsistencies and gaps in the law, removal of which would be indispensable to ensure the integrity of the legal system of the Republic of Poland*". In this context the question is surely to which competent law-making body the Tribunal sends such information. So far, it has been only the Senate, which in its Statute has inserted an additional chapter on the execution of Constitutional Tribunal's judgments.[325]

It is also significant, and well reflected in the Czech case law, that the notion of the so called "thick line" constituted a starting point both for the legislators to initiate new policies, and for the Constitutional Court to start constitutional review with a reference to the new, democratic constitution. This follows in a different method of adjudication techniques accepted by the Courts. While the Polish Constitutional Court accepted vast referential technique (it referred to the

---

324 Meaningful in this respect is the course of the first parliamentary debates over the significance and the use of the information of *The Substantial Problems* by the President of the Constitutional Court. For instance the issue of acceptance of the report was raised, as some of the MP's believed that the acceptance means an automatic transposition of the substance of the report and consequent work on it, in contrast to those who claimed that acceptance simply means acknowledging of the information. See for instance: the discussion on the information of the President of the Constitutional Court on *substantial problems arising from the activities and judgments of the Tribunal for the period from 1 January 1993 until 30 June 1994*, as provided for in the stenographic record of the debate in Sejm of the second term on its 43rd seating on 15 December 1995. It is also noticeable that the time for consideration of the information by the Parliament did not necessarily hold the deadlines, as provided for in the Statutes. See for example: the speech of the President of the Constitutional Tribunal, Andrzej Zoll in the Sejm on *substantial problems arising from the activities and judgments of the Tribunal for 1992* , as provided for in the stenographic record of the debate in Sejm of the second term on its 15th session (2nd day) on 18 March 1994. Both sources in the authors files but also available at: http://www.sejm.gov.pl/archiwum/arch2.html

325 Charter IXa on the execution of the Constitutional Tribunal's judgments was added to the Statute by Article 1 point 3 f the resolution of the Senate of 9 November 2007 (Mon. Pol., nr. 86, poz.925). The amendment entered into force on the same day.

transcripts of the discussions in the Parliament, legal literature, encyclopaedias, etc.) and axiological interpretation, the Czech Court preferred to assume that the substance is largely self evident from the constitutional formulation of a right, and its entourage by the principles. Of course, the Czech court defined the substances of given rights in its initial rulings. Still, they were less developed than the ones provided for by the Polish Court. The continuous reference to constitutional principles and to external sources of interpretation, were also a reason through which the Polish Tribunal sought legitimacy in socio-economic adjudication.[326] Undoubtedly, working under the *constitutional provisorium* was a challenge for the Constitutional Tribunal, which it used to establish its position in the domestic judicial and political system. On the other hand, the Tribunal is criticised of its extensive use and reference to constitutional values (as opposed to principles and constitutional norms derivative from the principles) as to the basis for assessing the compliance of laws with the Constitution. [327] The construction of the Court's decisions, especially of the so-called interpretative decisions that do not follow directly from constitutional provisions but reflect judge's own intellectual creation, expose the Court to allegations of political influence. A proper account of the interpretative decisions gives rise to doubts as to the issue of exclusive legislative competence of the Parliament and the independence of judges.[328] The problem of the interpretative decision with the universally binding force may be perhaps addressed by a turn to less frequently used signalling decisions provided that the responsiveness of the legislator is not only provided for in laws and regulations, but is a matter of an empirical fact.

326 The claim that the constitutional court continuously needs to prove its independence and autonomy is expressed in the doctrine by some constitutional lawyers. For example: Zdzisław Czeszejko-Sochacki, *Sądownictwo Konstytucyjne w Polsce na tle porównawczym*, Wydawnictwo Trybunału Konstytucyjnego, Warszawa, 2003, p.171 and further.

327 Zdzisław Czeszejko-Sochacki, *op.cit.*, p.185.

328 See: Marek Safjan, *Interpretacja a kontrola konstytucyjności*, Rzeczpospolita of 29 December 2003.

CONCLUSIONS

Martin Shapiro argued that the legitimacy of the judicial review and of courts in general, depends on their "triadic" character.[329] The logic of the triad is based on the idea that two parties in conflict refer their dispute to a third, neutral party for resolution. In order to give a full account of what judicial (constitutional) review is, the triadic model of dispute resolution needs to be accompanied by maintaining the consent both on the norm that will serve as a ground for settling the dispute, and on the judge, the third person who would find the facts and apply the norm previously agreed upon. Still, there is a risk that the moment the third party decides in favour of one of the disputants, the party to which the ruling was not in favour interprets the situation as a shift to a situation of two against one. Therefore, Shapiro supplements his concept by adding a "mediating continuum" that serves to provide communication and positions the third party as a mediator, arbiter. The triadic model mirrors the theory of constitutional dialogue. The theory of constitutional dialogue was referred to as an intra-institutional channelling of communication on the visions of materialisation of constitutional provisions, particularly on those that bind the state to undertake an action in socio-economic matters. Constitutional review is perceived, in this context, as being conducted to ensure democratic standards of decision-making rather than a means of guaranteeing "right answers" to socio-economic policy complexities.

With regard to the experience of the chosen Central Eastern European constitutions the discussion of the intra-institutional dialogue theory is preceded by an empirical study of their constitutional socio-economic case law. In fact, the analysis of the *acquis constitutionelle* of the three constitutional courts led to the observation that once constitutionalised socio-economic rights are a test for democracy. Not only can their material substance challenge the ways in which these rights can be materialised. It is also the procedural aspect that influences the inter-dependencies between the legislature, executive and constitutional judiciary, and thus sets up a space for a intra-institutional dialogue on the meaning of respective rights and the shaping of consequent social policies.

Upon examining the nature of socio-economic rights the question was whether the conventional understanding of constitutional socio-economic rights as moral rights gave a full account of their constitutional nature. It was argued that the analysis of legal, political, economic and moral justifications of the nature of socio-economic rights provides for a comprehensive set of features

329 Martin Shapiro, *Courts; a comparative and political analysis*, University of Chicago Press, Chicago 1981.

which, depending on convictions, account to considering them either as justiciable or non-justiciable. These considerations nevertheless omit an important feature of socio-economic rights which they gain once they are part of constitutions. What is missed in this picture is the influence these rights bear on the democratic decision-making based on constitutional provisions, such as the rule of law principle. Therefore, socio-economic constitutional rights not only address issues of social justice, solidarity, state responsibility or citizens' duties, but they play a pivotal role in the democratic intra-institutional dialogue, which is inscribed in the context of moral considerations. In this regard, socio-economic rights are considered as tools that serve to enhance the democratic standards of decision making.

This book discusses the nature of socio-economic rights followed by the analysis of constitutional formulation of these rights. The question is whether socio-economic rights can be constitutionalised, and if yes at what expense. The case of constitutional adjudication in the three Central Eastern European partly answers this question. The issue of justiciability was largely settled by the Constitutional Courts during constitutional changes in 1990s. Regardless of the textual formulation, especially well visible in case of the Polish Small Constitution, the Courts redefined the status of the said rights by referring to numerous constitutional principles, and *de facto* they have attributed the quality of judicial constitutional enforcement to these rights. Mostly, these rights gained features of indirect enforceability that requires a reference to procedural scrutiny of the challenged law, or to general constitutional clauses (such as social justice or equality). On the other hand, the Czech Constitutional Court largely accepted the vision of socio-economic rights as second generation, objective rights that are given limitations set in ordinary laws. In adjudication on socio-economic matters the Czech Court is largely influenced by the German doctrine that divides political and social rights. Slovak Constitutional Court accepted a more universal approach, although socio-economic rights are not directly applicable and subjected to limitations of ordinary laws. By and large, this study proves that the Courts tend to leave sufficient discretion to the legislator in finding means and resources to implement those rights by admitting that they will not judge the merits of the law but their constitutionality. The responsibility for materialisation of constitutional socio-economic rights is therefore shifted to the legislative and executive branch.

Constitutional socio-economic *acquis* from the three countries confirm that the Courts strive for a balance of constitutionality mandated by the democratic responsibility of the legislative. But is such a position well-founded or is it an example of opportunism? After all, the wide catalogue of socio-economic rights seems not to have a major transposition on the reality. If the final decisions are left entirely to the legislator who enjoys the democratic legitimacy? What is exactly the role of constitutional justice? Yet again, the principal cause of the weakness of constitutional adjudication in socio-economic matters, but perhaps not only in this field, stems from the fact that there is no communication, neither common interest shared by state actors to overcome potential deficiencies. The lack of communication is perhaps the most disturbing, since in this case every institution is left to realise its own, short-term interests. The legislators and the executive branch are interested in their political legitimacy, while the Courts fail to recognise the influence of its rulings in the long term perspective.

One of the Polish judges of the Supreme Administrative Court said that in fact the direct binding effect of the constitution requires that the legislator legislates in accordance with the constitution in force.[330] Therefore it is not only constitutional courts but also legislators who interpret the constitution. Certainly, the scope and mode of such interpretation is different. From this point of view it should be evident that the interpretation would vary, assumingly not so much on the substance of the rights but rather on the forms of their materialisation. This, in fact, brings in the controversy where different visions may conflict. As postulated in this book the *inherent and direct* obligation to rely on the constitution is a task of constitutional courts. The *external and indirect* precondition to ensure the respect of constitutional provisions rests on all other constitutional actors. This is why, the postulate of the intra-institutional dialogue may be considered as a means to redress the balance and enhance the importance of the long-term "constitutional thinking". In Poland, the foundations for the channelling of communication between the Tribunal and the legislative-executive branch are set up (yearly speech of the President of the Constitutional Tribunal in the parliament, the procedural regulation of the court-parliament contacts, a possibility to seek for information from the government on the potential consequences a ruling may have on the budget). In the Czech Republic and Slovakia, however, the separation of powers paradigm is much stronger. Yet, the potential of the constitutional dialogue (dialogue between national and EU courts) coming from the EU may contribute to the transposition of dialogue communication on national levels.

330 Lidia Błystak, *Czy Wystarczają instytucjonalne gwarancje sędziowskiej niezawisłości*, Rzeczpospolita Online, 30 November 2007, at www.rp.pl/artykul/72750.html. Justice Błystak said: "Despite of a direct regulatory force of the constitution, the ordinary judiciary is not exempted from the obligation to determine substantial norms that relate to constitutional values". (The text is available in Polish; the translation is the author's).

The reformulation of socio-economic rights in the Central Eastern European in democratisation context was chosen to challenge the conventional understanding of these rights as remnants of communism. It cannot be denied though that to a certain extent socio-economic constitutional rights are a relict of the past regimes. Nevertheless, as the historical analysis showed, there is a wider context of the constitutionalisation of socio-economic rights. Dealing with the past was an important aspect of giving a new meaning to constitutional socio-economic rights. It did not however prevent substantive problems that later the respective constitutional courts had to address.

Apart from discussing the wider context for the constitutionalisation of socio-economic rights, this book offers grounds for a broader contextualisation of debates on constitutional adjudication in social matters. An increasing awareness of the EU law influences national and also constitutional law, and is of great significance to the performance of national Constitutional Courts. After an extended period of relative neglect, constitutional socio-economic rights have gained considerable attention also at the EU level. Nowadays, it is not only the United Nations or the Council of Europe whose mechanisms foster the debates over the constitutionalisation of socio-economic rights. In fact, the growing attention to sustainable development has considerably advanced the European Union's endeavours to implement socio-economic rights within its primary laws. Throughout the analysis proposed here, the issue of the constitutionalisation of socio-economic rights and their consequent materialisation opens up the floor for a study of the ways in which EU law and jurisprudence influences the considerations of national constitutional courts over socio-economic rights, and if by any means it stimulates new dimensions of intra-institutional interactions in this field.

The contribution of this study also lies in re-conceptualising traditional debates over the nature of socio-economic rights. So far, the enforcement mechanisms were fundamentally important to these debates. However, in this respect, they do not offer a comprehensive explanation. The discussions on how to curtail courts preventing their activism shifted to the concept of the efficient mechanisms of institutional cooperation. This claim, being the main postulate of the dialogue theory, brings up an interesting and challenging aspect for discussion, not only at the national level in Europe, but also is worthy of consideration at the EU. Consequently, this book contributes to the debate on constitutional socio-economic rights by referring to the intra-institutional dialogue theory within the context of the conceptual change of constitutional socio-economic rights in the three Central Eastern European countries. It is claimed that the interactions of constitutional courts and other institutions contribute to the safeguarding and development of democratic decision-making. Particular attention was paid to the classic interaction between the constitutional judiciary, legislative and executive branches of the government. In light of the dialogue theory, the competences of these three actors differ, and subsequently their approach to the materialisation of constitutional socio-economic rights takes different forms. All things considered, the picture which is being drawn here shows a complex institutional set up, where the separation of powers is still treated as a fundamental precondition of the state being able to function but is not exclusively restricted to the attribution of specific powers to each constitutional actor. Instead, it provides for a network of inter-dependencies concentrated around one, common goal which is the materialisation of constitutional (socio-economic) rights.

It was not within the scope of this book to provide for an empirical study of the intra-institutional dialogue, but rather to indicate a possible, newly emerging tendency in constitutional adjudication. This novel approach has significant meaning with respect to socio-economic constitutional rights. It displays a global, holistic view that envisages the efficiency of laws and concentrates at the same time on institutional checks and balances. The principal grounds for this claim should be restated here. Firstly, the study of the case law shows that the legislative discretion in materialisation of socio-economic constitutional rights, recognised by the courts gives only a partial answer to the long-term interpretation of the constitutional meaning of a particular right. The difficulty in assessing a coherent vision of socio-economic constitutional rights is not only a matter for a consistent doctrine, but also for the coordination of intra-institutional efforts on their materialisation. Secondly, through the application of the dialogue theory the tensions between electorally accountable bodies and the constitutional judiciary in the allocation of authority when social policies are decided can be neutralised. Moreover, the practice shows that the determination of whether a particular case should be based on the axiological interpretation or rather on empirical grounds is troublesome when deciding upon socio-economic constitutional matters, especially with regard to constitutional norms. The focus on rational persuasion should be perhaps reinforced by the notion of efficiency which may be applied to constitutional programmatic norms. In these terms the efficiency of the programmatic norms is not only subject to the optimal interpretation of constitutional postulates but complies with the aim defined by these norms. That is to say, the materialisation of socio-economic programmatic norms that occur in the political context, also in light of the balancing of the decision-making costs, can be interpreted through the use of empirical data provided by experts, data analysis or the social context of the norm. In this respect it is assumed that the scope and straightforward examination during the abstract review of the constitutionality of norms improves the Court-legislator relation. The duty to clearly present the motives of a judgment is important for the legislator for future legal regulations resulting from the judgment.[331] The fact-based reasons for judicial decisions provide a clear motives that constitutional courts need in order to be able to consider consequences of their judgments. It also enhances the chances for a possible intra-institutional dialogue.

331 See: Marek Safjan, *Examining of facts in cases involving abstract control of normative acts*, Venice Commission Report: Law and Facts in Constitutional Jurisprudence, Vilnus, 30 June-1 July 2005, CDL-JU(2005)027.

Literature

Alexander L., *Are Procedural Rights Derivative Substantive Rights?*, Law and Philosophy, No. 17, 1998.

Alexy R., *Balancing, constitutional review, and representation*, International Journal of Constitutional Law, Vol.3, No.4, 2005.

Ambrož M., *The mediating role of the Ombudsman in the protection of human rights,* International Journal of Social Welfare, No.14, 2005.

Apodaca C., *Measuring Women's Economic and Social Rights Achievement*, 20 Hum. Rts. Quarterly, 1998.

Auleytner J., *Polityka społeczna, czyli ujarzmienie chaosu socjalnego*, Wydawnictwo Wyższej Szkoły Pedagogicznej TWP, 2002.

Banaszak B., *Prawa człowieka i obywatela w nowej konstytucji Rzeczypospolitej Polskiej*, Przegląd Sejmowy, No. 5(22), 1997.

Prawo konstytucyjne, Warszawa 2001.

Porównawcze prawo konstytucyjne współczesnych państw demokratycznych, Wolters Kluwer business, Warszawa 2007.

Banaszak B., Preisner A. (eds.), *Prawa i wolności konstytucyjne obywateli RP*Warszawa 2002.

Bateup C., *The Dialogic Promise. Assessing the Normative Potential of Theories of Constitutional Dialogue*, Brook. L. Rev., Vol. 71 Issue 3, 2006.

Bełdowski J., Metelska-Szaniawska K., *Law & Economic: Origins and Characteristics of the Economic Analysis of Law* (2007).

Blomquist W., Ostrom E., *Deliberation, learning and institutional change: the evolution of institutions in judicial setting*, Constitutional Political Economy, No. 19, 2008.

Blume L., Voigt S., *The Economic Effects on Human Rights*, Fachbereich Wirtschaftswissenschaften, UniKasselVersität, No.66/04.

Błystak L., *Czy wystarczają instytucjonalne gwarancje sędziowskiej niezawisłości*, Rzeczpospolita Online, 30 Nov/ 2007, at www.rp.pl/artykul/72750.html

Bobek M., *A new legal order, or a non-existent one? Some (early) experiences in the application of the EU law in Central Europe*, Croatian Yearbook of European Law and Policy, Vol.2, 2006.

Boudreaux D.J., Pritchard A.C., *Reassessing the role of the independent judiciary in enforcing interest-group bargains,* Constitutional Political Economy, Vol.5, No.1, 1994.

Brand D., *Introduction to socio-economic rights in the South African Constitution*, in: D. Brand, C. Heyns, *Socio-Economic Rights in South Africa,* Pretoria University Law Press, PULP, 2005.

Brennan G., Hamlin A., *A Revisionist View of the Separation of Powers*, Journal of Theoretical Politics, Vol.6, No.3, 1994.

Brennan G., Hartmunt Kliemt, *Logo Logic*, Constitutional Political Economy, Vol.1, No.1, December 1990.

Brzezinski M., *The Struggle for Constitutionalism in Poland*, Macmillan Press, St. Antony's College, Oxford 1998.

Buchanan J., *Constitutional Economics,* in: J. Eatwell, M. Milgate, P. Newman (eds.), *The New Palgrave- A Dictionary of Economics*, Vol. 1, Macmillan, London and Basingstoke 1987.

Freedom in Constitutional Contract- Perspectives of a Political Economics, Texas A&M University Press, College Station and London 1977.

The Constitution of Economic Policy, American Economic Review, vol. 77, No.3

The Independent Judiciary in an Interest-Group Perspective: Comment, Journal of Law and Economics, Vol.18, No.3, 1975.

The Limits of Liberty: Between Anarchy and Leviathan, University of Chicago Press, Chicago 1975.

Campbell R.W., *The Socialist Economies in Transition*, Indiana University Press, 1991.

Chruściak R., *The Small Constitution of 1992*, Przegląd Sejmowy, No. 5, 2007.

Chruściak R., Osiatyński W., *Tworzenie Konstytucji w Polsce w latach 1989-1997*, Instytut Spraw Publicznych, 2001.

Ciągwa J., *Rada Narodowa Republiki Słowackiej*, Wydawnictwo Sejmowe, Warszawa 1998.

Ciemniewski J., *Konstytucja państwa socjalnego czy liberalnego?,* in: *Prawo w okresie przemian ustrojowych w Polsce*, Warszawa 1995.

Sejm i Senat w projekcie Konstytucji RP, in: J. Krukowski (ed.), *Ocena projektu Konstytucji RP*, 1996.

Coomans F., *In Search of the Core Content of the Right to Education*, in: Audrey Chapman, Sage Russell (eds.), *Core Obligations: Building a Framework for Economic and Cultural Rights*, Insertia, Antwerp, Oxford, New York, 2002.

Some Introductory Remarks on the Justiciability of Economic and Social Rights in a Comparative Context, in: Fons Coomans (ed.), *Justiciability of Economic and Social Rights. Experiences from Domestic Systems*, 2006.

Cooter R.D., *The Strategic Constitution*, Princeton University Press, Princeton 1999.

Cooter R.D., Ginsburg T., *Comparative Judicial Discretion: An Empirical Test of Economic Models,* International Review of Law and Economics, Vol.16, Issue 3, 1996.

Cottrell J., Ghai Y., *The Role of Courts in the Protection of Economic, Social and Cultural Rights*, in: J. Cottrell, Y. Ghai (eds.), *Economic, Social and Cultural Rights in Practice*, 2004.

Cutler L., Schwartz H., *Constitutional Reform in Czechoslovakia: E Duobus Unum?*, University of Chicago Law Review, No. 58, 1991.

Czarny P., *Konstytucyjny status jednostki w państwie polskim*, in: P. Sarnecki (ed.), *Prawo konstytucyjne RP*, Warszawa 2002.

Czeszejko-Sochacki Z., *Sądownictwo Konstytucyjne w Polsce na tle porównawczym*, Wydawnictwo Trybunału Konstytucyjnego, Warszawa, 2003.

Čermakova Z., Holda D., Urbanek V., *Changes in Funding of Higher Education in the Czech Republic,* European Journal of Higher Education, Vol. 29, No.1, 1994.

Daintith T., *The constitutional protection of economic rights*, International Journal of Constitutional Law, Vol.2, No.1, 2004.

Davis D.M., *Socioeconomic rights: Do they deliver the goods?*, International Journal of Constitutional Law, 2008.

Deakin S., *Social Rights in a Globalized Economy*, in: Philip Alston (ed.), *Labour Rights as Human Rights*, 2005.

Den Exter A., *Legal Reforms of the Polish Health Care System in View of Accessing the European Union,* European Journal of Health Law, No. 8, 2001.

Den Exter A., Hermans B., *Constitutional Rights to Health Care: The Consequences of Placing limits to the Right to Health Care in several Western and Eastern European Countries*, European Journal of Health Law, No.5, 1998.

Derrida J., *Privilege: Justificatory Title and Introductory Remarks*, in: J. Plug (trans.), *Who's Afraid of Philosophy? Right to Philosophy I*, Stanford University Press 2002.

Dixon R., *Creating dialogue about socioeconomic rights: Strong-form versus weak-form judicial review revisited,* International Journal of Constitutional Law, Vol.5, No.3, 2007.

Drgonec J., *Ústava Slovenskej republiky. Komentár,* Heuréka 2004.

Základne práva a slobody podl'a Ústavy Slovenskej republiky. Zväzok 2, Manz, Bratislava 1999.

Działocha K. (ed.), *Basic Problems of Applying the Constitution of the Republic of Poland*, Sejm Publishing Office, Warsaw 2006.

Działocha K., Sarnecki P., Sokolewicz W., *Konstytucja Rzeczypospolitej Polskiej: Komentarz III*, Leszek Garlicki (ed.), Wydawnictwo Sejmowe, Warszawa, 2003.

Eide A., *Economic, Social and Cultural Rights as Human Rights*, in: Asbjørn Eide et al. (eds.), *Economic, Social and Cultural Rights*, 2001.

Realisation of Social and Economic Rights and the Minimum Threshold Approach, Hum. Rts. Law Jnl., No.10 1989.

Elcock H., *The Polish Ombudsman and the Transition to Democracy*, The International and Comparative Law Quarterly, Vol.45, No.3, 1996.

Elster J., *The Impact of Constitutions on Economic Performance*, in: *Proceedings from the Annual Bank Conference on Economic Development*, The World Bank, Washington 1995.

Ely J.H., *Democracy and Distrust. A Theory of Judicial Review*, Harvard University Press, 1980.

Evans A.J., *Constitutional moments in Eastern Europe and subjectivist political economy*, Constitutional Political Economy, No. 20, 2009.

Ewing K.D., *Social Rights and Constitutional Law*, Public Law, No. 104 , 1999.

Fabre, C., *Constitutionalising Social Rights*, 6 Journal of Political Philosophy, 1998.

Feld L., Voigt S., *Economic Growth and Judicial Independence: Cross Country Evidence Using a New Set of Indicators*, European Journal of Political Economy, Vo.19, No.3, 2003.

Flew A., *Equality in Liberty and Justice*, Routledge, 1989.

Florek L., *Zgodność przepisów prawa pracy z Konstytucją,* Praca i Zabezpieczenie Społeczne, No.11, 1997.

Forbath W.E., The Constitution and The Obligations of Government to Secure the Material Preconditions for a Good Society. Constitutional Welfare Rights: A History, Critique and Reconstruction, Fordham Law Review No.69, 2000-2001.

Frankowski S., *Lech Wałęsa's Draft of the Charter of Rights and Freedoms: An Overview,* Saint Louis – Warsaw Transatlantic Law Journal, No.65, 1996.

Freeman M., *Human Rights. An Interdisciplinary Approach*, Polity Press, Blackwell, 2002.

Friedman B., *Dialogue and Judicial Review,* Michigan L. Rev., No. 91, 1993.

Garlicki L., *Constitutional Law*, in: S. Frankowski (ed.), *Introduction to Polish Law*, 2005.

Polskie prawo konstytucyjne. Zarys wykładu, Warszawa, 2006.

Prawa socjalne w orzecznictwie Trybunału Konstytucyjnego, Przegląd Sejmowy, 1995.

Constitutional Courts versus Supreme Courts, International Journal of Constitutional Law, Vo.5, No.1, 2007.

Gevers S., *The Right to Health Care*, European Journal of Health Law, No.11 2004.

Granat M., *Sądowa kontrola konstytucyjności prawa w państwach Europy Środkowej i Wschodniej*, Wydawnictwo Sejmowe, Warszawa 2003.

Gronowska B., in: Z. Witkowski (ed.), *Prawo Konstytucyjne*, Toruń 1998.

Gutmann A., *Justice across the Spheres*, in: David Miller & Michael Walzer (eds.), *Pluralism, Justice and Equality*, 1995.

Henckearts J.-M., Van Der Jeught S., *Human Rights Protection Under the New Constitutions*

Hendriks A., *The Right to Health in National and International Jurisprudence*, European Journal of Health Law, No. 5, 1998.

Health Care and Positive State Obligations, European Journal of Health Law, No. 5, 1998.

Helman J.S., *Constitutions and Economic Reform: A Comparative Approach*, in: Jeffrey D. Sachs, Katharina Pistor (eds.), *The Rule of Law and Economic Reform in Russia*, Westview Press, Boulder, CO 1997.

Hempel C., Oppenheim P., *Studies in the Logic of Explanation*, Philosophy of Science, Vol.15, No.2

Hervey T., Kenner J. (eds.), *Economic and Social Rights under the EU Charter of Fundamental Rights- A Legal Perspective*, Hart Publishing, Oxford, Portland Oregon 2006.

Higley J., Lengyel G., *Elites after state socialism: theories and analysis*, Rowman & Littlefield, 2000.

Hirschl R., *Canada's Contribution to the Comparative Study of Rights and Judicial Review*, in: Linda A. White, Richard Simeon (eds.), *The Comparative Turn in Canadian Political Scene*, UBC Press, 2008.

Hogg P.W., Bushell A.A., *The Charter Dialogue Between Courts and Legislatures (Or Perhaps the Charter of Rights Isn't Such a Bad Thing After All)*, 35 Osgoode Hall Law Journal 75, 1997.

Holmes S., Sunstein C.R., *Koszt praw. Dlaczego wolność zależy od podatków*, Wydawnictwo Sejmowe, Warszawa 2003.

Jabłoński M., Jarosz-Żukowska S., *Prawa człowieka i systemy ich ochrony*, Wydawnictwo Uniwersytetu Wrocławskiego, Wrocław 2004.

Jaroń A., *Constitutional Courts as Actors of Fundamentalisation of Social Rights,* EUI Working Paper Law No. 2009/05, Florence, 2009.

Jičínský Z., *Ústava České republiky v politické praxi. Výběr článků a parlamentních vystoupení z let 1996-2006*, Linde Praha, Praha 2007.

Jíek D., Hoffmann M., *Czech Republic*, in: R. Blackburn, J. Polakiewicz (eds.), *Fundamental Rights in Europe. The European Convention on Human Rights and its Member States*, 2001.

Jowell, J., *Is Equalitz a Constitutional Principle?*, Current Legal Problems, No.47, 1994.

Katrougalos G. S., *The Implementation of Social Rights in Europe*, Colum. Jnl. European Law, 1996.

Kędzia Z., *Kryteria kształtowania konstytucyjnego katalogu praw, wolności i obowiązków człowieka i obywatela*, in: Zdzisław Kędzia (ed.), *Prawa, wolności i obowiązki człowieka i obywatela w nowej polskiej Konstytucji*, Poznańskie Centrum Praw Człowieka, Instytut Nauk Prawnych, Polska Akademia Nauk, Poznań 1990.

Klich A., *Human Rights in Poland: The Role of the Constitutional Tribunal and The Commissioner for Citizen's Rights*, St. Louis-Warsaw Transatlantic Law Journal 33, 1996.

Klima K., *La justice constitutionelle en Republique tchéque*, in: Marc Verdussen, *La justice constitutionnelle en Europe centrale. Centre d'études constitutionnelles et administratives*, Bruxelles, Paris, 1997.

Klug H., *Introducing the Devil: An Institutional Analysis of the Power of Constitutional Review*, South African Journal on Human Rights, No.13, 1997.

Koch I.E., *The Right to Education as a Means and an End in itself- the Indivisibility, Interdependence and Interrelation of human rights*, The Danish Institute for Human Rights 2001.

Kolodziej E.A., *A force profonde: the power, politics, and promise of human rights*, University of Pennsylvania Press, Philadelphia 2003.

Kornhauser L.A., *Appeal and Supreme Courts,* in: B. Bouckaert, G. De Gees (eds.*), Encyclopedia of Law and Economics*, Edward Elgar, University of Ghent, 1999.

Kornhauser L.A., *Judicial Organisation and Administration,* in: B. Bouckaert, G. De Gees (eds.*), Encyclopedia of Law and Economics*, Edward Elgar, University of Ghent, 1999.

Kumm M., *Constitutional rights as principles: On the structure and domain of constitutional justice*, International Journal of Constitutional Law, Vo.2, No.3, 2004.

Kusy M., *Human Rights Education, Constitutionalism and Their Interrelations in Slovakia*, European Journal of Education, Vol. 29, No.4, 1994.

Kühn Z., Kysela J., *Nomination of Constitutional Justices in Post-communist Countries: Trial, Error, Conflict in the Czech Republic*, European Constitutional Law Review, No. 2, 2006.

Landem W.M., Posner R.A., *The Independent Judiciary in an Interest-Group Perspective*, Journal of Law and Economics, Vol. 18, Issue 3, 1975.

Langford M., *Judging Social Rights*, Human Rights Tribune, Vol.11, No.3, 2006.

Judicial Enforcement of Economic, Social and Cultural Rights, Right to Food Journal, No. 2, 2003.

Lijphart A., *Democratization and constitutional choices in Czecho-Slovakia, Hungary and Poland. 1989 1991,* Wissenschaftszentrum Berlin, Berlin 1992.

Lityński A., *Historia Prawa Polski Ludowej*, Lexis Nexis, Warszawa 2008.

Łączkowski W., *Ekonomiczne i socjalne prawa człowieka a dobro wspólne*, in: *Godność człowieka a prawa ekonomiczne i socjalne. Księga jubileuszowa wydana w piętnastą rocznicę ustanowienia Rzecznika Praw Obywatelskich*, Warszawa 2003.

Łętowska E., *The Commissioner for Citizens' Rights in Central and Eastern Europe: the Polish Experience,* Saint Louis – Warsaw Transatlantic Law Journal, No.1, 1996.

Łopatka A., *Prawo człowieka- refleksje wokół pojęcia*, in: *Teoria prawa. Filozofia prawa. Współczesne prawo i prawoznawstwo*, Toruń, 1998.

Maciejczyk A., *Non-judicial system of socio-economic rights protection in Poland, the Czech Republic and Slovakia*, European University Institute, unpublished 2007.

Maciejczyk A., *Czy czeskie poplatky są konstytucyjne?*, Służba Zdrowia, No.22-25, 2008.

Malinowska I., *Instytucje ombudsmana w państwach Unii Europejskiej*, Przegląd Europejski, No.1, 2002.

Mann J.M. et al., *Health and Human Rights*, Health and Human Rights, No.1, 1994.

Manning N., *Social Needs, Social Problems and Social Welfare*, in: Pete Alcocl et al. (eds.), *The Student's Companion to Social Policy*, 2003.

Mathis K., *Efficiency Instead of Justice? Searching for the Philosophical Foundations of the Economic Analysis of Law,* Springer 2009.

Mazak J., *Review of Decisions of Ordinary Courts in Constitutional Complaint Proceedings Before the Constitutional Court of the Slovak Republic (Grasping the Nettle). Report,* European Commission for Democracy Through Law (Venice Commission), CDL-JU (2005)059, Strasbourg, 8 November 2005.

Meseznikov G., Kollár M., Nicholson T. (eds.), *Slovakia 2001: a Global Report on the State of Society*, Institute for Public Affairs, Bratislava 2002.

Metelska-Szaniawska K., *Konstytucyjne czynniki reform gospodarczych w krajach post-socjalistycznych. Studium empiryczne*, Uniwersytet Warszawski, Wydział Nauk Ekonomicznych, 2008.

Michelman F.I., *The Constitution, Social Rights, and Liberal Political Justification*, 1 Int. Journal Constitutional Law, 2003.

Mikłaszewicz P., *Obowiązki informacyjne w umowach z udziałem konsumentów na tle prawa w Unii Europejskiej*, Wolters Kluwer business, Warszawa 2008.

Mikosz J., *Prawo do nauki*, in: *Prawa człowieka. Model prawny*, Ossolineum 1991.

Mizerski R., *Kilka uwag o wolnościach i prawach w Konstytucji RP*, in: T. Jasudowicz (ed.), *Polska wobec europejskich standardów praw człowieka*, Toruń 2001.

Mołdawia T., (ed.), *Konstytucje Polskie 1918-2008*, Elipsa, Warszawa 2008.

Monahan P., *Politics and the Constitution: The Charter, Federalism and the Supreme Court of Canada,* Carswell, Scarborough 1987.

Mosca G., *The Ruling Class, McGraw-Hill*, New York, 1939.

Morawski L., *Główne problemy współczesnej filozofii prawa. Prawo w toku przemian*, Lexis Nexis, Warszawa 2005.

Moreau M.A., *Normes sociales, droit du traval et mondialisation. Confrontations et mutations*, Dalloz, 2006.

Mueller D.C., *Choosing a constitution in East Europe: Lessons from public choice*, Journal of Comparative Economics, Vol.15, Issue 2, 1991.

Constitutional Rights, Journal of Law, Economics, & Organisation, Vol.7, No.2, 1991.

Möller K., *Balancing and the structure of constitutional rights,* International Journal of Constitutional Law, Vol.5, No.3, 2007.

Murno C.R. , *Studies in Constitutional Law* , Butterworths LexisNexis, 2002.

Murray L., Phelan D.R., *La protection des droits sociaux fundamentaux dans l'ordre juridique de l'Irlande*, in : J. Iliopoulos-Strangas (ed.), *La protection des droits sociaux fundamentaux dans les Etats membres de l'Union européenne*, 2000.

Nagel T., *The Last Word*, Oxford University Press, 1997.

Nowak M., *The Right to Education*, in: Asbjørn Eide et al. (ed.*), Economic, Social and Cultural Rights – A Textbook*, Martinus Nijhoff Publ., The Hague 1995.

Office of the United Nations High Commissioner for Human Rights, *Economic, Social and Cultural Rights - Handbook for National Human Rights Institutions,* 2006.

Oniszczuk J., *Wolności i prawa socjalne oraz orzecznictwo konstytucyjne*, Szkoła Główna Handlowa w Warszawie, Warszawa 2005.

Osiatyński W., *An Argument against Popular Ratification and for Chancellor Democracy. Bronislaw Geremek on constitution-making in Poland. Interview with Bronisław Geremek,* EECR, Vol. 4, Nr.1, 1995.

Social and Economic Rights in a New Constitution of Poland, in: A. Sajo, *Western Rights? Post-Communist application*, 1996.

Rights in New Constitutions of East and Central Europe, Colum. Hum. Rts. L. Rev., 1994.

Wprowadzenie do praw człowieka, http://www.hfhrpol.waw.pl/pliki/WOsiatynski_HistIFilo.pdf

On Social and Economic Rights: A Needs-Based Approach, Bulletin of Transnational Center for Democratic Studies, Vo. 13/3, No. 45, 2003.

Human Rights for the 21st Century, Saint Luis - Warsaw Transatlantic Law Journal, No.29, 2000.

Palombella G., *From human rights to fundamental rights*, EUI Working Paper LAW No. 2006/34, Florence, 2006.

Pareto, V. *The Rise and the Fall of Elites*, *Totowa*, New York, 1968.

Pavlìček V. (ed.), *Ústava a ústavní řád České republiky. Komentář. 2. díl Práva a svobody*, Line, Praha 2002.

Persson T., Tabellini G., *The Economic Effects of Constitutions,* The MIT Press, Cambridge (Massachusets) and London 2003.

Pollitt Ch., Summa H., *Reflexive Watchdogs? How Supreme Audit Institutions Account for Themselves*, Public Administration, No. 75, 1997.

Procházka R., *Mission accomplished on Founding Constitutional Adjudication in Central Europe,* CEU Press, Budapest, New York 2002.

Přibáň J., Youg J., *The Rule of Law in Central Europe. The Reconstruction of Legality, Constitutionalism and Civil Society in the Post-Communist Countries,* Ashgate, Aldershot, Brookfield, Singapore, Sydney 1999.

Příbáň J., Roberts P.I., Young J., *Systems of justice in transition: Central European experiences since 1989*, Aldershot, Burlington Vt, Ashgate 2003.

Rapaczynski A., *Constitutional Politics in Poland: A Report on the Constitutional Committee of the Polish Parliament*, in: A.E. Dick Howard, *Constitution Making in Eastern Europe*, 1993.

Constitutional Politics in Poland: A Report on the Constitutional Committee of the Polish Parliament, University of Chicago Law Review, No.58, 1991.

Roach K., *Constitutional and Common Law Dialogues. Between the Supreme Court and Canadian Legislatures*, 80 Canadian Bar Review (Can. Bar. Rev.) 481, 2001.

Dialogic Judicial Review and its Critics, Supreme Court Law Review, No.23, 2004.

Rudak O., *Prawo do nauki*, in: B. Banaszak, A. Preisner (eds.), *Prawa i wolności konstytucyjne obywateli RP*, Warszawa 2002.

Sadurski W., *Conclusions: On the Relevance of Institutions and the Centrality of Constitutions in the Post-communist Transitions*, in: Jan Zielonka (ed.), *Democratic Consolidation in Eastern Europe*, 2001.

Constitutional Courts in the Process of Articulating Constitutional Rights in the Post-Communist States of Central and Eastern Europe. Part I: Social and Economic Rights, EUI Working Paper LAW No. 2002/14, Florence 2002.

Constitutional Socio-Economic Rights: Lessons from Central Europe, in: Workshop of the Foundation for Law, Justice and Society, Oxford 2008 (unpublished).

Human Rights and Fundamental Values, Archiv für Rechts-und Socialphilosohie, Beiheft 39, 1991.

Miętkość trybunalska, Gazeta Wyborcza, 7 December 2009.

Postcommunist Charters of Rights in Europe and the U.S. Bill of Rights, Law and Contemporary Problems, Vol. 65, No.2, 2002.

Postcommunist Constitutional Courts in Search of Political Legitimacy, EUI Working Paper LAW No. 2001/11, Florence, 2001.

Prawo przed sądem. Studium sądownictwa konstytucyjnego w postkomunistycznych państwach Europy Środkowej i Wschodniej, Warszawa 2008.

Rights Before Courts. A Study of Constitutional Courts in Post-communist States of Central and Eastern Europe, Springer, 2005.

Constitutional Theory, Aldershot, Burlington, VT: Ashgate/Dartmouth 2005.

Safjan M., *Interpretacja a kontrola konstytucyjności*, Rzeczpospolita of 29 December 2003.

Examining of facts in cases involving abstract control of normative acts, Venice Commission Report: Law and Facts in Constitutional Jurisprudence, Vilnus, 30 June-1 July 2005, CDL-JU(2005)027.

Politics- and Constitutional Courts (Judge's Personal Perspective), Polish Sociological Review, Issue 1(165), 2009.

Sajó A., *How the Rule of Law Killed Hungarian Welfare Reform*, E. Eur. Const. Rev., 1996.

Western Rights? Post-Communist Application, Kluwer Law International, 1996.

Salzberger E., Voigt S., *Separation of powers: new perspectives and empirical findings-introduction*, Constitutional Political Economy, No. 20, 2009.

Samuels W.S., *The Independent Judiciary in an Interest-Group Perspective: Comment*, Journal of Law and Economics, Vol.18, No.3, 1975.

Santera W., *Prawa (wolności) pracownicze w Konstytucji*, Praca i Zabezpieczenie Społeczne, No.11, 1997.

Schwartz H., *In Defence of Aiming High*, Fall East European Constitutional Review, 1992.

The Struggle for Constitutional Justice in Post-Communist Europe, University of Chicago Press, Chicago, London 2000.

Scott C., *Reaching Beyond (Without Abandoning) the Category of "Economic, Social, and Cultural Rights"*, 21 Hum. Rts. Quarterly, 1999.

Social Rights. Towards A Principled, Pragmatic Judicial Role, Economic and Social Law Review, Vo. 1 No.4, 1999.

The Interdependence and Permeability of Human Rights Norms: Towards a Partial Fusion of the International Covenants on Human Rights, 27 Osgoode Hall L.J., 1989.

Sen A., *Development as Freedom*, Oxford University Press, 1999.

Senevirante M., *Ombudsmen. Public Services and Administrative Justice*, Butterworths, LexisNexis, 2002.

Shapiro M., *Courts; a comparative and political analysis*, University of Chicago Press, Chicago 1981.

Shestack J.J., *The Philosophic Foundations of Human Rights*, Human Rights Quarterly, Vol.20, 1998.

Shue H., *Basic Rights: Subsistence, Affluence and US Foreign Policy,* Princeton University Press, 1980.

Sokolewicz W., *Nowa rola konstytucji w postsocjalistycznych państwach Europy*, Państwo i Prawo, No. 10, 2000.

Staśkiewicz W., *Stanowienie prawa*, in: Lena Kolarska-Bobińska (ed.), *Co warto, co należy zmienić? Poprawa jakości demokracji w Polsce*, Instytut Spraw Publicznych, Warszawa 2008; Wiesław Staśkiewicz, *Prawo jako narzędzie polityki państwa okresu przemian (przeszłość wobec przyszłości)*, in: Marek Zubik (ed.), *Prawo a polityka*, Liber, Warszawa 2007.

Stawecki T., Staśkiewicz W., Winczorek J., *Between Polycentrism and Fragmentation. The impact of Constitutional Tribunal Rulings on the Polish Legal Order*, Ernst and Young, Warsaw 2008.

Stein E., *Czecho/Slovakia. Ethnic Conflict, Constitutional Fissure, Negotiated Breakup*, University of Michigan Press, 1997.

Steiner H.J., *Social Rights and Economic Development: Converging Discourses?*, Buffalo Hum. Rts. L. Rev., No.4, 1998.

Steiner H., Alston P., *International Human Rights in Context. Law, Politics, Morals*, Oxford University Press, 2000.

Suchocka H., *Zakres i sposób regulacji praw ekonomicznych, socjalnych i kulturalnych a przyszłej konstytucji.*, in: Zdzisław Kędzia (ed.), *Prawa, wolności i obowiązki człowieka i obywatela*, 1990.

Sunstein C.R., *Against Positive Rights*, 2 East Europ. Const. Rev., 1993.

Something Old, Something New, East Europ. Const. Rev., No. 1, 1992.

Svák J., Cebulka L., *Ústavné právo Slovenskej republiky. Vybrané otázky, teorie, výučby a praxe,* Bratislavská vysoká škola práva, 2006.

Świątkiewicz J., *Rzecznik Praw Obywatelskich a sądownictwo administracyjne po reformie*, Biuro Rzecznika Praw Obywatelskich, 2004.

Syllová J. et.al., *Parlament České republiky,* Linde Praha, Praha 2008.

Taborsky E., *Czechoslovak Democracy at Work*, George Allen & Unwin, 1945.

Teubner G., *Societal Constitutionalism. Alternatives to State-centred Constitutional Theory*, Ius et Lex, 27 May 2004.

Titmuss R.M., *Commitment to Welfare*, Allen & Unwin., 1976.

Tremblay L.B., *The legitimacy of judicial review: The limits of dialogue between courts and legislatures*, International Journal of Constitutional Law, Volume 3, Number 4, 2005.

Trzciński J., *Komentarz do Art. 81 Konstytucji*, in: Lech Garlicki (ed.), *Konstytucja Rzeczypospolitej Polskiej. Komentarz*, 2003.

Konstytucja Rzeczypospolitej Polskiej. Komentarz, Vol. I, Warszawa 1999.

Tuori K., *Rights, Democracy and Lock Self-governancce: Social Rights in the Constitution of Finland,* Juridica International, No.2(70-73), 2007.

Tushnet M., *Judicial Activism or Restraint in a Section 33 World*, 52 University of Toronto Law Journal, 2003.

Policy Distortion and Democratic Debilitation: Comparative Illumination of the Countermajoritarian Difficulty, Michigan Law Review, Vol. 94, No.2, 1995.

Uitz R., *Constitutions, Courts and History*, CEU Press, 2005.

Viljoen F., *National Legislation as a Source of Justiciable Socio-economic Rights*, Social Economic Rights Review, No.6, 2005.

Voigt S., *Constitutional Law*, in: B. Bouckaert, G. De Gees (eds.), *Encyclopedia of Law and Economics*, Edward Elgar, University of Ghent, 1999.

The economic effects of judicial accountability: cross-country evidence, European Journal of Law and Economics, No. 25, 2008.

Positive Constitutional Economics II- A survey of Recent Developments, MAGKS Papers on Economics 2009 36, Philipps-Universität Marburg, Faculty of Business Administration and Economics, Department of Economics, 2009.

Waldron J., *A Right-Based Critique of Constitutional Rights*, Oxford Journal of Legal Studies, No.13, 1993.

Wesson M., *Grootboom and Beyond: Reassessing the Socio-Economic Jurisprudence of the South African Constitutional Court*, South African Journal on Human Rights, No.20, 2004.

Wieruszewski R., *National Implementation of Human Rights*, in: A. Rosas, I. Helgesen (eds.), *Human Rights in a Changing East/West Perspective*, London, 1990.

Wierzchowska I., *Koncepcja i ewolucja historyczna praw społecznych*, in: J. Ciapała, K. Flaga-Gieruszyńska (eds.), *Prawa podmiotowe. Pojmowanie w naukach prawnych*, Szczecin, 2006.

Winczorek P., *Axiological Foundations of the Constitution of Poland*, Saint Louis – Warsaw Transatlantic Law Journal, No.59, 1997.

Wiśniewski L., *Prawo a wolność człowieka- pojęcie i konstrukcja prawna*, in: L Wiśniewski (ed.), *Podstawowe prawa jednostki i ich ochrona sądowa*, Warszawa 1997.

Zakres i konstrukcja praw socjalnych w przyszłej konstytucji RP, in: L. Wiśniewski (ed.), *Podstawowe prawa jednostki i ich ochrona sądowa*, Warszawa 1997.

Zakolska J., *Zasada proporcjonalności w orzecznictwie Trybunału Konstytucyjnego*, Wydawnictwo Sejmowe, Warszawa 2008.

Zemánek J., *The Emerging Czech Constitutional Doctrine of European Law*, EuConst, No. 3, 2007.

Zubik M. (ed.), *Konstytucja III RP w tezach orzeczniczych Trybunału Konstytucyjnego i wybranych sądów*, C.H. Beck, Warszawa 2008.

Księga XX-lecia Orzecznictwa Trybunału Konstytucyjnego, Biuro Trybunału Konstytucyjnego, Warszawa 2006.

Selected Constitutional Case Law Polish Constitutional Tribunal

U 7/01, *Constitutional Tribunal Judgment of 2 July 2002*, published in: Dz.U. 2002.104.933 of 11 July 2002.

K 11/00, *Judgment of 4 April 2001* ,"eviction to nowhere case" (*eksmisja na bruk)*

SK 18/99, *Judgment of 8 November 2000* on tuition fees for studies, Z.U.2000/7/258; Dz.U.2000.101.1091 of 23 November 2000.

P 12/99, *Judgment of 15th November 2000* concerning principles of judicial control of decisions on extradition of foreigners from the Republic of Poland, published in: Dz.U. 2000.100.1085 of 21 November 2000.

SK 22/99, *Constitutional Tribunal Judgment of 8 May 2000*, published in: Dz.U. 2000.38.438 of 12 May 2000.

P 11/98, *Judgment of 12 January 2000*, concerning "regulated rents" in private buildings, Dz.U. 2000.3.46 of 21 January 2000.

SK 9/98, *Judgment of 15 May 1999*, concerning the easement appurtenant, Dz.U. 1999.49.498 of 31 May 1999.

P 2/98, *Judgment of 12 January 1999*, concerning lawlessness in construction, Dz.U. 1999.3.30 of 15 January 1999.

K 8/96, *Judgment of 17 July 1996*, OTK ZU No. 5/1996.

K 7/95, *Judgment of 19 November 1996*, OTK ZU No. 6/1996.

K 11/95, *Judgment of 26 April 1995*, OTK part 1, 1995.

W 3/93, *Resolution of 2 March 1994*, OTK part 1, 1994, p.158, **W 8/93**, *Resolution of 16 march 1994*, OTK pArt.1 1994.

K 14/92, *Judgment of 19 October 1993* concerning employment and pensions provision

K 14/92, *Judgment of 19 October 1993*, OTK part 2, 1993.

K 1/91, *Judgment of 28 May 1991*, OTK 1991.

K 14/91, *Judgment of 11 March 1992* concerning disability and old-age pensions.

S 1/91, *Signalling Decision of 13 February 1991*, concerning the case K 11/90 of 30 January 1991, Z.U. 1991// 29; OTK 1986-1995/t3/1991/29.

K 7/90, *Judgment of 2 August 1990* concerning pension provision for employees and their families OTK 1990.

K 1/88, *Judgment of 30 November 1988* on pension provision for employees and their families- Solidarity of Work Veterans.

Czech Constitutional Court

Pl. ÚS 2/08, *Judgment of 23 April 2008* on public finance reform (sickness-leave benefits)

Pl. ÚS 24/07, *Judgment of 31 January 2008* on public finance reform (procedural and taxation matters)

Pl. ÚS 77/06, *Judgment of 15 February 2007- přilepky*

IV. ÚS 158/04, *Judgment of 4 April 2005*

III. ÚS 252/04, *Judgment of 25 January 2005*

II.ÚS 405/02, *Judgment of 3 June 2004 - employment abroad*

Pl. ÚS 2/02, *Judgment of 9 March 2004- Basic Principles*

II. ÚS 405/02, *Judgment* of *3 June 2003*

Pl. ÚS 35/95, *Judgment of 10 July 1996*, Patients' out-of-pocket payments case

ÚS 35/93, Published under 49.1994 Sb

Slovak Constitutional Court

PL. ÚS 5/93 (unpublished; copy with the author)

PL. ÚS 26/06, *Judgment of 30 April 2008* concerning exemption of health care benefits

PL. ÚS 16/06, *Judgment of 30 April 2008* on suspension of benefits

PL. ÚS 16/05, *Judgment of 2 July 2008* on directory of medical services, concerning reimbursement of health services by public health insurance

Lex et Res Publica
Polish Legal and Political Studies

Edited by
Anna Jarón

Vol. 1 Anna Jarón: Socio-Economic Constitutional Rights in Democratisation Processes. An Account of the Constitutional Dialogue Theory. 2012.

www.peterlang.de